Series/Number 09-169

ORDINAL ITEM RESPONSE THEORY

Mokken Scale Analysis

Wijbrandt H. van Schuur
University of Groningen, The Netherlands

Los Angeles | London | New Delhi
Singapore | Washington DC

Los Angeles | London | New Delhi
Singapore | Washington DC

FOR INFORMATION:

SAGE Publications, Inc.
2455 Teller Road
Thousand Oaks, California 91320
E-mail: order@sagepub.com

SAGE Publications Ltd.
1 Oliver's Yard
55 City Road
London EC1Y 1SP
United Kingdom

SAGE Publications India Pvt. Ltd.
B 1/I 1 Mohan Cooperative Industrial Area
Mathura Road, New Delhi 110 044
India

SAGE Publications Asia-Pacific Pte. Ltd.
33 Pekin Street #02-01
Far East Square
Singapore 048763

Copyright © 2011 by SAGE Publications, Inc.

Printed in the United States of America

Library of Congress Cataloging-in-Publication Data

Schuur, Wijbrandt van

Ordinal item response theory : Mokken scale analysis /
Wijbrandt H. van Schuur.

p. cm.—(Quantitative applications in the
social sciences; 169)
Includes bibliographical references and index.

ISBN 978-1-4129-8804-9 (pbk. : acid-free paper)

1. Social sciences—Methodology. 2. Social sciences—
Research. I. Title.

H62.S355 2011
001.4'2—dc22
2011000512

This book is printed on acid-free paper.

11 12 13 14 15 10 9 8 7 6 5 4 3 2

Acquisitions Editor: Vicki Knight
Associate Editor: Lauren Habib
Editorial Assistant: Kalie Koscielak
Production Editor: Brittany Bauhaus
Copy Editor: Carol Anne Peschke
Typesetter: C&M Digitals (P) Ltd.
Proofreader: Sue Irwin
Indexer: Diggs Publication Services, Inc.
Cover Designer: Candice Harman
Marketing Manager: Helen Salmon
Permissions Editor: Adele Hutchinson

Quantitative Applications in the Social Sciences

A SAGE PUBLICATIONS SERIES

Quantitative Applications in the Social Sciences

A SAGE PUBLICATIONS SERIES

CONTENTS

ABOUT THE AUTHOR

Wijbrandt H. van Schuur is associate professor at the Faculty of Behavioral and Social Sciences of the University of Groningen, The Netherlands. He is interested in measurement models and has taught measurement and scaling models in Groningen and at the Essex Summer School in Social Science Data Analysis. He has developed an ordinal unidimensional unfolding model and a model for the ordinal circumplex (for the first see *Political Analysis*, 1993, and *Applied Psychological Measurement*, 1994; and for the second, *Essays in item response theory: Lecture notes in statistics, Vol. 157*, 2001). His main substantive research interest is in the measurement of political knowledge (e.g., *Acta Politica*, 2000), and, in collaboration with the Documentation Centre Dutch Political Parties, the study of party membership (e.g., *Research in Political Sociology, Vol. 18,* 2010).

SERIES EDITOR'S INTRODUCTION

In his landmark 1958 book *Theory and Methods of Scaling,* psychophysicist Warren Torgerson distinguished *fundamental measurement* from what he termed *measurement by fiat.* Measurement by fiat assigns numbers to objects arbitrarily, with the assignment typically justified by an appeal to reasonableness or common sense. A widespread example of this kind of measurement is Likert or summated-rating scaling, in which serial integers are assigned to ordered categories—such as 1 to Strongly Disagree, 2 to Disagree, 3 to Agree, and 4 to Strongly Agree—and the numbers are summed across several items to compose a scale. There is no deep justification for the assumption that the item categories are equally spaced or that it makes sense to sum the scores for the items, although in introducing this approach Rensis Likert did make an effort to demonstrate that different assignments of numbers to categories produce very highly correlated scales. The properties of summated-rating scales, such as reliability, are the subject of *classical test theory.*

Torgerson's book concerned itself in contrast with methods of fundamental measurement in psychology and the social sciences, including methods that later evolved into *item-response theory.* For numbers to be assigned to objects in fundamental measurement, the numbers must be shown to obey certain rules. For example, in an ordinal scale, it must be demonstrable that if one object is assigned a higher number than another, the object with the higher number has more of the property being measured. Similarly, to justify an interval scale, it is necessary to demonstrate that equal differences in scale values represent equal differences in amounts. Another way of putting it is that models for fundamental measurement make strong claims about the structure of measurements, claims that are capable of being falsified by data.

The simplest item-response models concern dichotomous items in which individuals are, in the terminology of Clyde Coombs's seminal 1964 book *A Theory of Data*, in a *dominance relation* to the items—for example, questions on an exam. Whether an individual gets an exam question right is a function both of the individual's knowledge or ability and the item's level of difficulty. It is assumed in such models that individuals and items can be placed on a common dimension of ability and difficulty. In the deterministic Guttman-scale model, for example, an individual will necessarily get a question correct if his or ability exceeds the difficulty of the item, and wrong if it does not. Probabilistic item-response models—such as the normal-ogive model discussed by Torgerson, and the similar logistic model introduced in 1960 by the Danish psychometrician Georg Rasch—are more nuanced: The probability of getting an item right increases smoothly as a function of the difference between an individual's ability and the difficulty of the item.

Since the time of Guttman, Torgerson, Rasch, and Coombs there has been a flowering of item-response theory. Although Wijbrandt van Schuur discusses a variety of item-response models in the current monograph, including Guttman scales and Rasch models, the monograph focuses on *ordinal* item-response models for dichotomous and ordered items—precisely the kind of data that have traditionally composed summated-rating scales. The models do not assume that the probability of response is a normal, logistic, or any other specific joint function of the positions of the response and an individual on an underlying scale. Instead, the item-response function is simply constrained to be monotone. These models, originally introduced by the Dutch statistician and social scientist Robert J. Mokken, yield ordinal scales.

By weakening the assumption that item-response curves take a particular functional form, ordinal item-response theory offers the possibility of composing more realistic scales that will fit a wider variety of data in the social and behavioral sciences. van Schuur does an admirable job of explaining the background, justification for, and structure of ordinal item-response models. I anticipate that his monograph will lead to the increased use of these models by researchers and consequently to the improvement of social measurements.

–John Fox
Series Editor

ACKNOWLEDGMENTS

The authors and SAGE would like to acknowledge the contributions of the following reviewers:

David Andrich, *The University of Western Australia*

William G. Jacoby, *Michigan State University* and *ICPSR*

For Eric Tanenbaum, former director of the
Essex Summer School in School Social Science
Data Analysis and Collection.
Always at the forefront of methodological innovation.

CHAPTER 1. INTRODUCTION

1.1 The Problem of Measurement in the Social Sciences

In our daily conversations we often refer to characteristics of people that are difficult to observe. We may say of a person that "he is very active," "she is very intelligent," or "he is more conservative than his wife." We conclude this after observing a specific instance of activity, intelligence, or conservatism. But we do not leave it at that; we generalize. We assume that these observations tell us something about characteristics, or traits, of people that go beyond specific instances. A person who behaves actively, intelligently, or conservatively now will (we believe) also behave this way later. Some people are (we believe) more active, more intelligent, or more conservative than others in general. And social scientists would like to be able to measure such personality traits or characteristics. Because these traits can only be inferred by observing specific instances of behavior, we call them *latent* traits. Latent traits stand in contrast to *manifest* traits, that is, characteristics that can be observed directly and (usually) do not change, such as gender or ethnic background.

Social scientists are often interested in latent traits such as abilities (e.g., level of activity, knowledge, or intelligence) or attitudes (e.g., conservatism, trust, or religious beliefs). They believe that abilities and attitudes are important in explaining why people behave the way they do, why they make the choices they make. This makes the social scientist's work difficult because these characteristics of people are hard to measure. Social science would be much easier if the units of measurement used were simpler, along the lines of monetary units or units from the natural sciences, such as blood pressure, electric potential in the brain, or the chemical composition of blood.

An additional problem is that most latent traits that social scientists want to measure do not have well-established units of measurement. For instance, there is no such thing as the milli-Marx as a unit of alienation or the kilo-Freud as unit of frustration. Social scientists have not been able to build social microscopes or telescopes. They can use numerical (or cardinal, or interval level) measurements only if they are willing to accept a number of restricting assumptions. They may need to settle for measurement at the ordinal level, that is, ordering people with respect to their ability or attitude. In such a case we will call the measurement instrument an *ordinal scale,* sometimes also called a nonmetric or nonparametric scale.

1.2 Measurement Theory and
Item Response Theory for Dichotomous Items

We may even wonder whether it is possible to measure latent traits such as abilities and attitudes. The answer to this question is yes, but only if we are prepared to accept certain assumptions. These assumptions are formulated in a theory. Because most of our measurement depends on the interpretation of answers to test or survey questions, *our assumptions deal with a theory about how people answer questions.* One such theory is known as item response theory (IRT). The questions are called items, and the behavior of a person (i.e., his or her answer to a question) is called the response. The simplest behavior is the dichotomous response, which allows only two options. For instance, a person either has or has not performed a certain activity; she has given the right or the wrong answer to a knowledge question; he has agreed or disagreed with a conservative statement. IRT is formalized in a mathematical (measurement) model. This is not as ominous as it sounds. In fact, every step in understanding this model is quite simple.

We will first pursue the possibilities of measuring latent traits of people on the basis of only dichotomous responses. Once the measurement model for dichotomous responses is explained, we will extend it to a measurement model that allows more than two possible responses. For ease of exposition we will refer to a dichotomous item as having two responses: a positive response and a negative response. Which of the two responses the researcher calls positive depends on the direction of the latent trait she wants to measure (e.g., activity rather than inactivity, knowledge rather than lack of knowledge, conservatism rather than liberalism) and has no moral connotations.

1.3 Two Fundamentally Different IRT Models

We can distinguish between two fundamental reasons why people may give the positive ("yes") response to an item. Let me explain this with an example of two different sets of questions that can both be answered with "yes" or "no."

1a. Are you approximately 1.80 m (5'11") tall?	yes/no
1b. Are you approximately 1.70 m (5'7") tall?	yes/no
2a. Are you at least 1.80 m (5'11") tall?	yes/no
2b. Are you at least 1.70 m (5'7") tall?	yes/no

All four questions include a size as some kind of benchmark. To questions 1a and 1b a person gives the positive response only if indeed he is approximately 1.80 m or 1.70 m tall. The height of the person is the same as the height that is mentioned in the question. Or, to say it slightly differently, the difference between the height of the person and the height mentioned in the question is negligible, and their similarity or proximity is high. In contrast, the negative response is ambiguous: A person who is not approximately 1.70 tall is either shorter or taller; these two possibilities are each other's opposite.

Each person who says "yes" to question 2a or 2b can have any height greater than 1.80 m or 1.70 m. Moreover, there is an overlap in the groups of people who give the positive response to questions 2a and 2b because anyone who is taller than 1.80 m necessarily is taller than 1.70 m. Relations such as "greater than" or "taller than" are called dominance relations. Similarity relations, as described in the previous paragraph, are called proximity relations.

On the variable height, all people can be represented with a number: their value, that is, their height, in centimeters or in feet and inches. But—and this may be difficult to grasp at first—each of the questions, or items, can also be represented with a number or value: the benchmark value implied in the question. Questions 1a and 1b receive the positive response from a person who has (approximately) the same number as the item. Questions 2a and 2b receive the positive response from a person who has a higher number than the item. A positive response to questions 1a and 1b is called a *proximity* response, and a positive response to questions 2a and 2b is called a *dominance* response.[1]

---

[1]Proximity responses may seem useless because of the ambiguity of the negative response. But there are situations—for instance in analyses of preferences, child development, or politics—in which it is useful to ask questions that lead to responses that are best analyzed as proximity responses. In those cases the negative response will have one of two opposite meanings. For example, "Do you like coffee with one lump of sugar?" ("No, I like coffee without sugar," or "No, I like coffee with more sugar"). "Does the baby crawl?" ("No, the baby cannot crawl yet," or "No, the baby does not crawl anymore"). "Is voting the only way for people to have a say in government?" ("No, voting is not a way," or "No, there are more ways"). Such data cannot be analyzed with the model described in this monograph. However, they can be analyzed with an IRT measurement model called the unfolding model, which was invented by Coombs (see Coombs, 1950, 1964; and some of his successors, e.g., Andrich & Luo 1993; Roberts, Donoghue, & Laughlin, 2000). An ordinal unfolding model, analogous to the model discussed in this monograph, was developed by van Schuur (1993) and van Schuur and Kiers (1994). Circular unfolding models, also known as the circumplex (e.g., Plutchik & Conte, 1997), have been developed by Browne (1992) and others. An ordinal circular unfolding model has also been developed (Mokken, van Schuur, & Leeferink, 2001).

This chapter will deal only with dominance responses and with an IRT model that represents them: *the dominance model.* It is sometimes called the Guttman scale, after its originator, Louis Guttman (1950).

There are two classes of dominance models: metric and ordinal. The difference is that in metric models we take the values with which people and items are represented as numbers on an interval scale, whereas in ordinal models we interpret these values only in terms of their rank order, that is, as numbers on an ordinal scale. This monograph deals only with the ordinal dominance model (for metric models, see Andrich, 1988; Bond & Fox, 2007; Embretson & Reise, 2000; Ostini & Nering, 2006; Smith & Stone, 2009). We will get back to the implications the ordinal model has for the use of scale scores in linear multivariate statistical techniques, such as regression analysis or analysis of variance, in chapter 9.

CHAPTER 2. THE GUTTMAN SCALE

2.1 A Special Relation Between the Members of a Pair of Questions

In order to understand the principle behind Guttman scale analysis, we will compare the answers to the two members of several pairs of questions. Let us call the two questions of each pair question A and question B. For example,

Height	
Question A: Are you taller than 1.70 m?	yes/no
Question B: Are you taller than 1.80 m?	yes/no
Arithmetic Ability	
Question A: Did the student give the right answer to 2 + 2?	yes/no
Question B: Did the student give the right answer to 23 * 17?	yes/no
Political Ideology	
Question A: Should income differences be decreased?	yes/no
Question B: Should income differences be abolished?	yes/no
Religious Belief	
Question A: Do you believe in heaven?	yes/no
Question B: Do you believe in hell?	yes/no
Affluence	
Question A: Do you own a CD player?	yes/no
Question B: Do you own a dishwasher?	yes/no

These five pairs of questions have something in common. In each pair more people say "yes" to A than to B. Moreover—and this is important—for each pair, if people say "yes" to B, they will generally also say "yes" to A. This last statement is logically true only for the first pair of questions. If people are taller than 1.80 m, then they must be also taller than 1.70 m. But for the other four pairs this relationship between A and B does not always hold. Still, surveys show that a person who gives the "yes" answer to B usually gives the "yes" answer to A. I will deal with exceptions to this relationship later, but for now assume that for each of these four pairs of questions the relationship exists.

How do we explain the fact that a person who agrees with question B also agrees with question A? The general answer is that both questions in a pair give us an indication of the value of a person on a more general variable that underlies their responses. This is the clearest for the first pair. If people are taller than 1.80 m, their measurement value, or scale value, on a variable height will be greater than 1.80 m. If they are not taller than 1.70 m, their height value will be lower than 1.70 m. And if people are taller than 1.70 m but not taller than 1.80 m, then their height value will be between 1.70 m and 1.80 m.

The same principle applies to the second pair of questions. We take the responses to both questions to depend on an underlying variable that we may call arithmetic ability. A person has to have more arithmetic ability to answer B correctly than to answer A correctly. So these two questions can be used to classify people as belonging to one of three categories (i.e., as having one of three scale values) on this underlying variable:

0: They cannot answer either question correctly.

1: They can answer only question A correctly.

2: They can answer both questions correctly.

The difference between this example and the first is that there are instruments to measure people's height directly but not to measure their arithmetic ability. We cannot connect a person to some mechanical or electric measuring device in which a dial or a digital reading shows how much arithmetical ability they have. If we want to measure someone's arithmetic ability, then we must use indirect indicators such as questions A and B. If someone is less likely to give the correct answer to the more difficult question B than to the easier question A, we can say that the correct answer to B implies the correct answer to A. A Guttman scale with such questions is therefore sometimes called an *implicational scale*. From this implication it follows that there will be more people who give the positive response to A than to B. We will use the term *easier* for the more popular question (i.e., the question with more positive responses) and the term *more difficult* for the less popular question in a pair of questions (i.e., the question with fewer positive responses). So in all our examples so far A was easier and B was more difficult.

The third pair of questions deals with political opinions. The opinion expressed in question B can be considered more extreme than the opinion expressed in question A. Agreeing with either statement about income differences implies that one wants the income differences to be reduced. But people who agree with question B want to go even further than that. So the answers to the two questions separate people into three groups:

0: People who believe that income differences should not be reduced

1: People who believe that income differences should be reduced but not abolished completely

2: People who believe that income differences should be abolished altogether

The variable that is indirectly measured with the two questions is often called political ideology, or, more specifically, the socioeconomic left–right dimension or the liberal–conservative dimension. Because variables such as arithmetic ability and political ideology cannot be directly observed, they are often called unobserved variables, meaning that they are unobserved by any kind of direct measurement instrument. The two questions, A and B, are called indicators of the unobserved variable.

Another term that is used instead of *unobserved variable* is *latent variable.* The term *latent* seems to suggest that the variable is not really there but only pops up when the relevant indicator questions are asked. As mentioned earlier, rather than speaking of a latent variable, some psychometricians talk about a latent trait, in which a trait is a fixed personality characteristic. Such substantive interpretations of unobserved variables are not necessary for the Guttman scale to be applicable. Often these different terms are used interchangeably without reference to their psychometric meaning.

The fourth pair of questions deals with religious beliefs. People who believe in hell turn out also to believe in heaven, whereas not everyone who believes in heaven also believes in hell. We may interpret the answers to these two questions in terms of degree of religious belief. The two questions allow us to classify people into three categories (or give them scale values on the unobserved variable degree of religious belief):

0: People with no (or little) religious belief (do not believe in heaven or hell)

1: People with some religious belief (believe in heaven but not in hell)

2: People with stronger religious belief (believe in both heaven and hell)

The fifth pair of questions deals with affluence. Many people own a CD player, but, at least in the northern part of the Netherlands in 1997, only a minority of people owned a dishwasher (Sanders & van Schuur, 1998).

Nevertheless, people who own dishwashers generally also own CD players. So these two questions classify people into three categories (or give them scale values on the unobserved variable degree of affluence):

0: Not very affluent (not even a CD player)

1: Somewhat affluent (only a CD player)

2: More affluent (both a CD player and a dishwasher)

2.2 Using Answers to Questions as Measurement

Each of the five pairs of questions mentioned earlier can be used as an instrument to make a rather coarse measurement (i.e., to classify people into one of three groups). The measurement values are ordinal, which means we know that the measurement value on the variable we measure increases from one group to the next, but we don't know how much it increases.

Measurement values, or scale values, can be given to each subject simply by adding the number of "yes" answers to the two questions. This gives us the classification into three groups with the numbers 0, 1, and 2. For an ordinal scale this classification is identical to giving the groups the numbers 1, 2, and 3, which might seem more sensible at first. The classification (0, 1, 2) is simply used for reasons of convenience. The lowest value is always zero, and the highest value is identical to the number of questions. The value "1" in this classification implies that question A—the easier question—was answered positively and question B—the more difficult question—was not. We will deal later with situations that do not conform to this model (i.e., in which B was answered positively but A was not).

2.3 Ordinal Measurement With More Than Two Items

For each of these five examples we might add an unlimited number of other questions measuring the same latent variable. For example, subject's height can be assessed with questions using other numbers, like the following:

Question C: Are you taller than 1.75 m?	yes/no

Adding this question allows us to split the group of subjects whose height was between 1.70 m and 1.80 m into two groups: one between 1.70 m and 1.75 m and the other between 1.75 m and 1.80 m. Adding this third question allows the subjects to be classified into four groups.

The scale values of the members of each of these four groups—0, 1, 2, and 3—are *measurements*. Admittedly, they are not obtained with a ruler, but they are measurements according to the general definition of measurement: "The assignment of numbers to objects in such a way that the relations between the objects are represented by the relations between the numbers" (Coombs, Dawes, & Tversky, 1970, p. 12). The relations between objects—the subjects, in this example—is the relation between their relative height (some are taller than others). And the relation between the numbers is simply the order relationship: The numbers are ordered from 0 to 3, hence the term *ordinal scale*. So ordering subjects and items is a form of measurement, be it a weaker form than measurement with a ruler. In chapter 3 the consequences of this idea will be elaborated.

Similarly, arithmetic ability can be measured more finely by adding more questions, such as these:

Question C: Did the student give the correct answer to: (237 * 21)/28?	yes/no
Question D: Did the student give the correct answer to: (13.267 * 108.936)/2.67?	yes/no

If we can assume that the four questions, A, B, C, and D, are ordered in terms of increasing difficulty, then a person giving the correct answer to question D will also give the correct answer to questions C, B, and A.

For these four questions, let us now make a small dataset, with all the appropriate responses: the code "1" will mean "the answer was correct" and the code "0" will mean "the answer was incorrect." If the items are ordered from easy to difficult, and the subjects are ordered from less to more able, then the data matrix shows a lower triangle with the positive responses and an upper triangle with the negative responses. Such a structure was called a scalogram by Guttman.

items →:	A B C D
subjects ↓:	
0	0 0 0 0
1	1 0 0 0
2	1 1 0 0

(Continued)

(Continued)

3	1 1 1 0
4	1 1 1 1

Questions about political ideology (the third example) can be extended by adding questions about other forms of equality, such as question C: Should men and women earn the same amount of money if they have the same job? (yes/no).

Let us assume (as we find in empirical research) that more people agree with question C than with question A (and therefore with question B). By analogy with the example of arithmetic ability, we will call question C *easier* or *less difficult* than questions A and B. This terminology is sometimes confusing when it is applied to questions that have nothing to do with arithmetic ability. In this context the meaning of the terms *easy* and *difficult* simply indicates how many people will give the positive (in our examples, "yes") answer to the question.

To extend the pair of questions about religious beliefs, we can add more "Do you believe in . . . ?" questions (or items, as these questions are often called). For example,[1]

Question C: Do you believe in God?	yes/no
Question D: Do you believe in life after death?	yes/no

And to extend the "affluence scale" we can use questions about additional possessions, for instance,[2]

Question C: Do you own a color printer?	yes/no
Question D: Do you own a microwave oven?	yes/no
Question E: Do you own a car?	yes/no

---

[1] A larger battery of such questions is used in the European and World Values Study.

[2] It turned out that eight questions could be asked such that if people owned a certain apparatus or performed a certain activity (that is, if they gave the positive response to that question), then they would also give the positive response to the easier items (Sanders & van Schuur, 1998).

The scales discussed here are often called *cumulative scales*.[3] Subjects with increasing scale values have accumulated more of the latent variable.

2.4 The Guttman Scale: The Perfect Deterministic Cumulative Scale

All is well as long as people who give the positive response to a difficult dichotomous item also give a positive response to all easier dichotomous items. If this is the case, we call the set of items a *deterministic cumulative scale*. A deterministic scale does not contain any response patterns that go counter to the scale and is therefore sometimes called a perfect scale.

Let us now formally introduce the deterministic model with some notation and graphical representation. We will show what it means for two dichotomous items, **i** and **j**, to have different benchmarks or thresholds along the continuum that represents a latent trait. If we interpret this continuum as a single new variable, that is, a single new theoretical concept, then we will represent it by a single horizontal line. The dichotomous items are represented by their positions along the line; these positions indicate their benchmarks. Positions of *items* will be indicated by the Greek symbol δ (delta), so item **i** is denoted as δ_i, and item **j** is denoted as δ_j. Each person is also represented by a position on the latent continuum. For people, also referred to as *subjects*, we will use the Greek symbol θ (theta). The "general" subject (subject **s**) will be denoted by θ_s. Subject **s**'s response to item **i** places **s** in one of two areas along an underlying latent continuum: The response "0" places **s** to the left of δ_i, and "1" places **s** to the right of δ_i. This is shown in Figure 2.1.

Figure 2.1 Item **i** divides the latent continuum into two parts.

---

[3]The use of terms such as *cumulative scale* or *implicational scale* differs between scientific disciplines.

12

If there is a second dichotomous item, **j**, with another scale value, δ_j, subject **s** can be given a second representation along the continuum, as shown in Figure 2.2.

Figure 2.2 Item **j** divides the latent continuum into two parts.

If we display both items simultaneously, we get the representation in Figure 2.3.

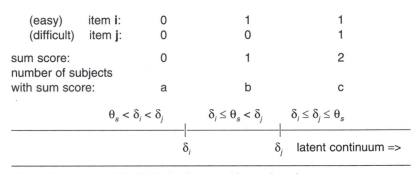

Figure 2.3 Items **i** and **j** divide the latent continuum into three parts.

The information in Figures 2.1, 2.2, and 2.3 can be summarized in a cross table, with item **i** in the rows and item **j** in the columns (Table 2.1). The number of subjects with sum score 0 (a) are represented in cell (0,0), those with sum score 1 (b) in cell (1,0), and those with sum score 2 (c) in cell (1,1). There are no subjects with the scores 0 for item **i** and 1 for item **j**. The cell (ij,01) is empty in the perfect, deterministic cumulative scale. The empty cell is called the *error cell*. The scale value of each subject is defined as the number of items to which he or she gives the positive (1) response.

2.5 Assumptions of the Deterministic Model

The deterministic model we have described so far can be summarized in terms of a few assumptions.

First, the latent trait to be measured is a single trait, and it can be represented as a unidimensional continuum.

		Item **j**		
		0	1	Total
Item **i**	0	a	0	a
	1	b	c	b + c
Total		a + b	c	a + b + c

Table 2.1 Cross table of two perfectly cumulative dichotomous items. Cells contain frequency of response to both items **i** and **j**.

Second, subjects with a scale value lower than the scale value of an item will give the negative response to that item, and subjects with a scale value at least as high as or higher than that of the item will give the positive response to that item.

Third, the probability of giving the positive response to each item depends only on the value of the subject on the latent trait, and not on any other systematic influence (i.e., the assumption of local stochastic independence).

2.6 Louis Guttman and the Guttman Scale

The dominance model has been known for a long time under such names as *cumulative scale analysis, implicational scale analysis,* and *Guttman scaling.* It was developed by sociologist Louis Guttman in World War II (for more information about the Guttman Scale in this QASS series, see Andrich, 1988; Jacoby, 1991; or McIver & Carmines, 1981). As a member of a group of social scientists, Guttman (1950) was asked to assess the quality and morale of the American soldiers. He designed survey questions for soldiers that asked about their fear in combat, their attitude toward officers, and other such issues.[4] Guttman's "fear of combat" scale contained questions like these:

---

[4]Guttman believed that it would be better for variables to have only two answers or response categories (e.g., yes/no, agree/disagree) rather than five, for ease of responding. Some items are genuinely dichotomous, such as questions with correct and incorrect responses. But in surveys, items are often *made* dichotomous by collapsing three or more response categories into two. For example, if questions (often called items) have five possible responses, such as 1 = *agree very much,* 2 = *agree somewhat,* 3 = *uncertain,* 4 = *disagree somewhat,* and 5 = *disagree completely,* they can be dichotomized by recoding 1 and 2 as 1 = *agree* and 3, 4, and 5 as 0 = *don't agree.* The response with the code "1" is generally called the positive response, and the response with the code "0" is the negative response.

How often did you have the following reactions when you were under fire:

A. Sinking feeling in the stomach   often/not often

B. Vomiting   often/not often

C. Urinating in pants   often/not often ("often" is the
                                      positive alternative)

Guttman's "attitude toward officers" scale contained question like these:

A. How do you feel about the privileges that officers get compared with those that enlisted men get?

1. Officers have far too many privileges; 2. Officers have a few too many privileges; 3. Officers have about the right number of privileges; 4. Officers have too few privileges. (Positive alternative: 1 and 2)

B. Do you feel that your officers recognized your abilities and what you were able to do?

1. Yes, I'm sure they did; 2. Yes, I think they did, but I'm not sure; 3. No, I don't think they did; 4. Undecided. (Positive alternative: 3)

C. How many of your officers used their rank in ways that seemed unnecessary to you?

1. Almost all of them; 2. Most of them; 3. Some of them; 4. Only a few of them; 5. None of them. (Positive alternative: 1 and 2)

Unfortunately, the perfect deterministic Guttman scale hardly exists in social scientific research situations. So it is to the imperfect scale that we will now turn.

CHAPTER 3. THE IMPERFECT
CUMULATIVE SCALE

3.1 Model Violations

If a set of items does not form a perfect Guttman scale but contains a few "wrong" responses, we do not necessarily need to discard it. A "wrong" response, or a "model violation," "model error," or simply "error," is a response that is inconsistent with the implications of the model. Guttman's scaling model is very restrictive. With k dichotomous items, there are 2^k possible response patterns in total, but only $k + 1$ response patterns form a perfect Guttman scale. So with 8 dichotomous items, there are $2^8 = 256$ possible response patterns but only 9 acceptable patterns. It is highly unlikely, even with the best possible set of questions, that a dataset contains only these nine acceptable response patterns. We therefore need to consider how to define *model violation* and how many model violations can be accepted.

In the 1950s and 1960s there was much discussion about how to define the number of errors or model violations for response patterns with more than two items. Take, for instance, the response pattern ABCD,1101 to the items A, B, C, and D, in which A, B, C, and D are ordered from the easiest to the most difficult. Are there two errors, because item C should be answered positively and item D should be answered negatively, if the number of positive responses is kept constant? Or is there only one error, because changing the response of either C or D would make the pattern perfect?

To add to this confusion, we also have to ask whether we still can use the response pattern ABCD,1101 for measurement purposes and, if so, how. Should such a person get the scale value 2 because her response pattern can be made perfect by changing the response to item D to 0? Should she get the scale value 4 because her response pattern can be made perfect by changing the response to item C to 1? Or should she get scale value 3 because she gave the positive response to three items? An excellent review of this debate can be found in chapter 2 of Mokken (1971). We return to this question later in this chapter.

3.2 Error: Violation of a Transitivity
Relation Between Items and Subjects

The answer a person gives to a question is interpreted as a dominance relation between the person and the question (the item). The person dominates the item if she gives the positive response, and the item dominates the person if she gives the negative response. If we have more people and more items, and if all people and items can be represented along a single dimension, we can infer two other types of dominance relationships, namely dominance relations between people and dominance relations between items. This is the case because when all people and items can be represented along a single dimension, all these dominance relations are transitive. And if all dominance relations are transitive, then we have managed to order both the people and the items with respect to each other along that dimension. The concept of a model violation, or an error, can therefore best be explained as the violation of a transitivity relation.

Let us assume three items, A, B, and C, in order of difficulty, and four subjects, W, X, Y, and Z, in order of ability (Figure 3.1):

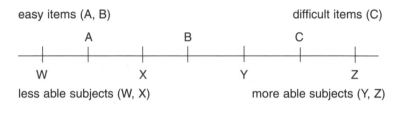

Figure 3.1 Four subjects (W, X, Y, Z) and three items (A, B, C) along a cumulative scale.

1. We can specify a transitivity relationship *between three items* as follows: If item B is more difficult than item A, and if item C is more difficult than item B, then item C is more difficult than item A. This transitivity relationship is logically true if we define the "easiness"— and hence also the "difficulty"—of an item by the frequency (or proportion, as the relative frequency) of people who give the positive response to that item. If two or more items have exactly the same proportion of positive answers, we cannot order them, and they are tied. In terms of Table 2.1, both cells (0,1) and (1,0) should then be empty. But if the proportion of people agreeing with each item differs, then we have found the order of the items based on their "popularity" or, conversely, "difficulty."

Now we can specify three other transitivity relationships.

2. *Between two people and one item.* If person Y is more able than item B is difficult (i.e., if person Y is represented to the right of item B on

the dimension), and if person X is less able than item B is difficult (i.e., person X is represented to the left of item B), then person Y is more able than person X. This transitivity relationship (Y > B, B > X, and therefore Y > X) is used to order two people in terms of their ability, or scale value, on the dimension. The outcome of this transitivity relationship can then be used in the third transitivity relation.

3. *Between three people.* If person Y is more able than person X, and if person Z is more able than person Y, then person Z is more able than person X. This transitivity relationship allows us to give rank orders as scale values to all people (i.e., to give scale values on an ordinal scale to these people).

There is a fourth kind of transitivity relationship that is crucially important.

4. *Between one person and two items.* If person Y is more able than item B is difficult, and if item B is more difficult than item A, then person Y is also more able than item A is difficult. In other words, if person Y can give the positive response to the difficult item B, then he should also be able to give the positive response to the easy item A. Note that I purposely write *should,* because it is not always true that if a person gives the positive response to a difficult item, he also gives the positive response to an easier one.

Only the last of these four transitivity relations can logically be violated. We therefore define a model violation as *the violation of the transitivity relationship between one person and a pair of items.* Each time a person gives the positive response to a difficult item and the negative response to any easier item, she violates the cumulative model; that is, she makes an error with respect to the deterministic cumulative model. That is why this error is sometimes called a *Guttman error.* The number of errors a person makes in the response pattern ABCD,1101 is therefore 1, because only item pair (pair CD) violates the model.[1]

Let us see how to calculate the number of errors in the following response patterns (in which the items are given in order of difficulty from

---

[1]Establishing the number of model violations is possible only if we have established the difficulty order of the items. Previous definitions of model violations in terms of changing responses such that perfect patterns occur imply that such changes may affect the difficulty order of the items. However, this is not the case when model violations are defined in terms of a transitivity relationship between a subject and two items. In practical applications of this model the researcher may either use a preestablished theoretical order of the items or experiment with different possible orders of difficulty. We will not pursue this theme further in this monograph and will assume that the difficulty order of the items is known.

left to right). With four items there are six—namely 4*(4–1)/2—item pairs. The number of model violations is the number of item pairs that violate the model. Table 3.1 gives some examples. The order of the items was previously established by their order of difficulty in the sample, where A is the easiest and D is the most difficult item. In the first response patterns (ABCD,0011) four of the six item pairs violate the model. The number of model violations in this response pattern, or of a subject who gives this response pattern, therefore is four.

ABCD	AB	AC	AD	BC	BD	CD	
0 0 1 1	0	1	1	1	1	0	4 errors: item pairs AC, AD, BC, BD
0 1 1 1	1	1	1	0	0	0	3 errors: item pairs AB, AC, AD
0 1 0 1	1	0	1	0	0	1	3 errors: item pairs AB, AD, CD
0 0 0 1	0	0	1	0	1	1	3 errors: item pairs AD, BD, CD
1 0 1 1	0	0	0	1	1	0	2 errors: item pairs BC, BD
0 1 1 0	1	1	0	0	0	0	2 errors: item pairs AB, AC
1 0 0 1	0	0	0	0	1	1	2 errors: item pairs BD, CD
0 0 1 0	0	1	0	1	0	0	2 errors: item pairs AC, BC
1 1 0 1	0	0	0	0	0	1	1 error: item pair CD
1 0 1 0	0	0	0	1	0	0	1 error: item pair BC
0 1 0 0	1	0	0	0	0	0	1 error: item pair AB
# of violations	4	4	4	4	4	4	24 model violations in this (hypothetical) dataset

Table 3.1 Comparison of item pairs that violate the cumulative model of four items in order from least to most difficult (1: violation; 0: no violation).

3.3 Extension of the Definition of Error to a Larger Dataset

When the number of errors in the response pattern of one subject has been defined as the number of item pairs in that response pattern that violate the cumulative model, it is easy to define the total number of errors in the dataset: It is simply the sum of the number of errors over all subjects. So if the dataset consists of the 11 response patterns in Table 3.1 then the total number of errors in the dataset would be 24, calculated either from the last column or from the last row.

We can also calculate the number of errors contributed by each item separately. Knowing the number of errors in each item will turn out to be helpful in a later stage of developing a cumulative scale or evaluating whether all items in a cumulative scale are equally good. Although we need an item pair to define an error, we can distinguish the members of the pair by attributing an error in the pair to each of the two items separately. The number of errors for each item is then defined as the total number of item pairs that involve that item and that contain an error, summed over all people.

A small example is given in Table 3.2. Whereas in Table 3.1 we compared each item pair, in Table 3.2 we look at individual items by combining the item pairs that contain them. Item A consists of item pairs AB, AC, and AD, item B consists of item pairs AB, BC, and BD, and so on. For subject 1 with response pattern 0001, three item pairs violate the model: AD, BD, and CD. So items A, B, and C are each involved once, and item D is involved three times. Rather than showing all 11 response patterns with four items that contain one or more errors, here we show only five such patterns.

Errors in item (i.e., in item pairs containing that item)							
	ABCD	*A*	*B*	*C*	*D*	*Total*	*Item pairs*
Person 1	0 0 0 1	1	1	1	3	3	AD, BD, CD
Person 2	0 1 1 1	3	1	1	1	3	AB, AC, AD
Person 3	1 0 0 1	0	1	1	2	2	BD, CD
Person 4	1 0 1 1	0	2	1	1	2	BC, BD
Person 5	0 0 1 0	1	1	2	0	2	AC, BC
Total		5	6	6	7	12	

Table 3.2 Calculating the number of errors in each item separately.

3.4 How Can We Evaluate the Amount of Model Violation in a Dataset?

Now that we have established what we mean by a model violation or a model error, and we can calculate the number of such errors, how do we evaluate the amount of error? What do we mean by "not too many errors"? Here again, a number of different answers have been given in the literature, and again Mokken's (1971) book provides an excellent overview. If we can compare the number of errors we observe with some benchmark, we may be able to express the amount of model error in a measure of model fit. Several measures of model fit, which we may call criteria for scalability, have been proposed. We will discuss some of the major ones now.

What is the benchmark against which we want to compare the number of errors in the dataset? One answer that comes to mind is to use the maximum number of errors possible for this dataset. But what is the maximum number of errors that people can make?

The worst situation would be the one in which every person gave a positive response to all the difficult items and a negative response to all the easy items, as in ABCD,0011. But in almost all empirical situations the difficulty of the item is established from the very dataset under study. So if everybody gave the response ABCD,0011, items C and D would automatically be defined as the easy items and A and B as the difficult ones. In such a situation the maximum number of errors could never be as high as the total number of responses, the number of people times the number of items ($N * k$). In fact, it is not easy to determine the maximum number of errors possible in a dataset. A number of procedures give us estimates of that number, but these can be proven to overestimate the real maximum number of errors.

If we were able to determine the maximum number of errors possible, then we could develop a criterion for scalability by comparing the number of errors observed to the maximum number of errors. The first criterion for scalability developed by Guttman was called *the coefficient of reproducibility*, **Rep**.

$$\text{Rep} = 1 - \frac{\text{Err(obs)}}{N * k} \tag{3.1}$$

Here, Err(obs) is the observed number of errors and $N * k$ is the total number of responses. **Rep** can therefore be interpreted as the proportion of responses not in error.

In later proposed criteria for scalability, $N * k$ was replaced by a better estimate of the maximal number of model violations, Err(max). *The coefficient of scalability* **S** was then defined as follows:

$$\mathbf{S} = 1 - \frac{\text{Err(obs)}}{\text{Err(max)}} \qquad (3.2)$$

But even if we had a proper estimate of the maximum number of errors, we have another reason for not wanting to compare the number of errors observed with the maximum number of errors. This problem can best be understood if we think of establishing the criterion for scalability as a form of hypothesis testing. We generally test one hypothesis by comparing it with another hypothesis. One hypothesis is that our dataset does indeed form a cumulative scale. But what should the other hypothesis be? When we compare the number of errors that we have observed with the maximum number of errors possible, given a candidate ordering of the items, we are saying in essence that the other hypothesis is that the data conform to a model that is as different from a cumulative scale as possible. But how sensible is this as the other hypothesis?

A more appropriate other hypothesis is the null hypothesis, according to which the items are simply unrelated. They do not form a cumulative scale, nor do they conform to some other weird extreme model. If the items are unrelated, we cannot predict whether someone who gives the positive response to a supposedly difficult item will give the positive response to a supposedly easier item. Or, put differently, our prediction about whether a person gives the positive response to an easy item does not change if we know that he responded positively to a more difficult item.

The idea that we should compare the number of errors observed with the number of errors expected *under statistical independence,* Err(exp), was suggested by Loevinger in 1948 but not taken up until the end of the 1960s by Mokken. Mokken reintroduced Loevinger's *coefficient of homogeneity* **H** as a criterion for scalability:

$$\mathbf{H} = 1 - \frac{\text{Err(obs)}}{\text{Err(exp)}} \qquad (3.3)$$

Here, Err(exp) for item pair **(i,j)** is the number of errors expected under statistical independence, and Err(obs) is the number of subjects who give both a positive response to the more difficult item **j** and a negative response to the easier item i.[2] $H = 1$ implies perfect model fit, because then there are no errors to be observed. That is also true when $Rep = 1$ or when $S = 1$. $H = 0$ implies that we cannot distinguish our dataset from a completely random dataset. H can be negative when we observe more errors then we would expect under statistical independence. This might happen, for instance, if we used the wrong order of difficulty of the items.

So let us compare the following two hypotheses:

| The null hypothesis | H_0 | The items are unrelated. |
| The model hypothesis | H_1 | The items form a cumulative scale. |

It is common practice in statistics to want to reject or falsify the null hypothesis in favor of the model hypothesis. The model hypothesis is generally called the alternative hypothesis. To put this strategy of model testing more informally, everything worse than perfect is bad, but everything better than random is good.

The easiest way to describe the number of errors expected under statistical independence is by reference to a cross table of two items. As an example, let us return to the two questions about religious beliefs:

| Question A: Do you believe in heaven? | yes/no |
| Question B: Do you believe in hell? | yes/no |

Let us assume that in interviews with 100 people, we find that 24 people believe in heaven and hell, 34 believe in neither heaven nor hell, 36 believe in heaven but not hell, and 6 believe in hell but not heaven (Table 3.3a). Do these two items form a cumulative scale? Let us compare the number of errors observed with the number of errors expected under statistical independence.

---

[2]Err(exp) is calculated as $[1 - p(i)]*p(j)*N$, in which $p(i)$ and $p(j)$ are the relative frequencies with which the positive response to these items were given, and N is the sample size of the dataset. H has the same interpretation as Goodman and Kruskal's (1979) coefficient λ (lambda) as a proportional reduction in error measure. It can also be interpreted as the ratio of the correlation between the two variables over the highest possible correlation, given the marginal distributions of the two variables.

		Heaven		
		Yes	No	Total
	Yes	24	6	30
Hell	No	36	34	70
	Total	60	40	100

Table 3.3a Hypothetical empirical situation: Belief in heaven versus belief in hell.

How do we find the number of errors observed? In the 2×2 cross table in which the row item is the difficult one (only 30 positive answers) and the column item is the easier one (60 positive responses), the upper right top cell (hell yes, heaven no) can be called the error cell. In a perfect cumulative scale, this cell is empty, as in the second cross table (Table 3.3b), called the perfect situation. In the empirical situation, however, the error cell contains 6 people, that is, Err(obs) = 6.

		Heaven		
		Yes	No	Total
	Yes	30	0	30
Hell	No	30	40	70
	Total	60	40	100

Table 3.3b Perfect Guttman scale for items from Table 3.3a.

How do we find the number of errors expected under statistical independence? In the case of statistical independence the probability of a given response to two items is simply the product of the probability of the response to each item taken separately. So if the probability of a positive response to the difficult item is 0.30 and the probability of a negative response to the easy item is 0.40 (1 − 0.60), the probability of the two responses taken together is 0.3 * 0.4 = 0.12. Because there are 100 people in the dataset, we expect 100 * 0.12 = 12 people to give the error response to these two items if the items are statistically independent. Therefore, Err(exp) = 12 (Table 3.3c).

		Heaven		
		Yes	No	Total
Hell	Yes	18	12	30
	No	42	28	70
	Total	60	40	100

Table 3.3c Cross table if response to items from Table 3.3a were statistically independent.

Now we can compute the coefficient of homogeneity for this scale of two items:

$$H = 1 - \frac{6}{12} = 0.50$$

Note that if the denominator Err(exp) becomes 0, it will be impossible to calculate the **H** value. Err(exp) becomes 0 if all subjects give the positive response to the easier item or if all subjects give the negative response to the more difficult item. Items to which every subject gives the same response are therefore not included in the analysis.

The coefficient of homogeneity is 0.50. Now the next question is, "Is this high or low?"

3.5 Evaluating the Coefficient of Homogeneity

There are two ways to approach the question, "How high or low is a coefficient of homogeneity **H** = 0.50?" Informally, we might ask, "How close is 0.50 to 0.00?" or no homogeneity, or we might ask, "How close is 0.50 to 1.00?" or perfect homogeneity. There is a statistical answer to the first question. It is possible to estimate the probability that a certain value of the coefficient of homogeneity (say, our 0.50) in a sample of size N is found in a population that has an **H** coefficient of 0.00, which means that the responses to all items are unrelated. This statistical answer is given in Appendix 1. It depends on finding the distribution of the **H** coefficient, in the case that all responses are statistically independent, and deriving a (one-sided) confidence interval between 0 and a positive value, given a particular exceedance probability α (generally

5%). If **H** falls within this confidence interval, we accept the null hypothesis and reject the model hypothesis that our items form a cumulative scale. This decision is formulated in terms of a Z and a $Z(i)$ statistic, Z for the whole scale and $Z(i)$ for item i: If Z (or $Z(i)$) is high enough (roughly >3), then the homogeneity of the whole scale (or of item i) cannot be explained by chance.

But accepting the model hypothesis—that the coefficient of homogeneity is higher than 0.00 in the entire population—does not provide an answer to the second question: How high is high, or how close is our dataset to perfect homogeneity? Unfortunately, there is no simple answer to this question. Correlations, or coefficients of homogeneity, that are statistically significant may still not be very important. Mokken has suggested that datasets with coefficients below 0.30 are not homogeneous enough to form a cumulative scale. He based this suggestion on substantive experience and informal comparison with scales accepted on the basis of reliability and factor analysis.

3.6 Using the Coefficient of Homogeneity in Scales With More Than Two Items

Now that we can test whether two items form a cumulative scale by interpreting the coefficient of homogeneity, we can extend this test to scales with more than two items. In such a scale we sum the number of errors observed, Err(obs), in each item pair. So with four items, we add over the six pairs. We can also calculate the amount of error expected under statistical independence, Err(exp), for each item pair and sum over all item pairs. The coefficient of homogeneity for the whole scale, **H**, is as follows:

$$\mathbf{H} = 1 - \frac{\sum\limits_{i=1}^{k-1} \sum\limits_{j=i+1}^{k} \mathrm{Err(obs)}}{\sum\limits_{i=1}^{k-1} \sum\limits_{j=i+1}^{k} \mathrm{Err(exp)}} \tag{3.4}$$

Let us give an example with four items in Tables 3.4 and 3.5:

Item A × Item B

Item A	Item B		
	Yes	No	
Yes	25	5	30
No	25	45	70
	50	50	100

Item A × Item C

Item A	Item C		
	Yes	No	
Yes	24	6	30
No	36	34	70
	60	40	100

Item A × Item D

Item A	Item D		
	Yes	No	
Yes	26	4	30
No	54	16	70
	80	20	100

Item B × Item C

Item B	Item C		
	Yes	No	
Yes	40	10	50
No	20	30	50
	60	40	100

Item B × Item D

Item B	Item D		
	Yes	No	
Yes	43	7	50
No	37	13	50
	80	20	100

Item C × Item D

Item C	Item D		
	Yes	No	
Yes	52	8	60
No	28	12	40
	80	20	100

Table 3.4 Example with four items.

Item pair	AB	AC	AD	BC	BD	CD	Sum
Err(obs)	5	6	4	10	7	8	40
Err(exp)	15	12	6	20	10	12	75
H	0.67	0.50	0.33	0.50	0.30	0.33	0.47

Table 3.5 Summary of the results from Table 3.4.

The sum of the errors *observed* over all item pairs is $5 + 6 + 4 + 10 + 7 + 8 = 40$.

The sum of the errors *expected* over all item pairs is $15 + 12 + 6 + 20 + 10 + 12 = 75$.

$$\mathbf{H} = 1 - \frac{40}{75} = 0.47$$

It is now also possible to determine the coefficients of scalability of each of the four items, A, B, C, and D. In this case the number of errors observed and expected have to be summed over the item pairs that include the item under scrutiny.

$$\mathbf{H_A} = 1 - \frac{5 + 6 + 4}{15 + 12 + 6} = 1 - \frac{15}{33} = 0.55 \quad \mathbf{H_B} = 1 - \frac{5 + 10 + 7}{15 + 20 + 10} = \frac{22}{45} = 0.51$$

$$\mathbf{H_C} = 1 - \frac{6 + 10 + 8}{15 + 20 + 12} = 1 - \frac{24}{47} = 0.49 \quad \mathbf{H_D} = 1 - \frac{4+7+8}{6 + 10 + 12} = \frac{19}{28} = 0.32$$

Each of the four items has a coefficient of homogeneity that is higher than the proposed lower boundary of 0.30. It is easy to show that when each of the items in a cumulative scale has a coefficient of homogeneity larger than some value c, the scale as a whole will also have a coefficient of homogeneity that is larger than c. The inspection of the coefficient of homogeneity of individual items allows the researcher to evaluate these items for their inclusion in the cumulative scale. Items that are not sufficiently homogeneous should not be part of a cumulative scale. Item D, for instance, just barely makes the lower boundary of 0.30. Table 3.6 gives another numerical example.

Number of errors in a cumulative scale										
A	B	C	D	Freq.	AB	AC	AD	BC	BD	CD
1	1	1	1	70						
1	1	1	0	240						
1	1	0	1	40						40
1	0	1	1	20				20	20	
0	1	1	1	8	8	8	8			
1	1	0	0	160						
1	0	1	0	60				60		
1	0	0	1	28					28	28
0	1	1	0	16	16	16				
0	1	0	1	14	14		14			14
0	0	1	1	4		4	4	4	4	
1	0	0	0	168						
0	1	0	0	48	48					
0	0	1	0	24		24		24		
0	0	0	1	10			10		10	10
0	0	0	0	90						
---	---	---	---	----	--	--	---	--	--	--
726	596	442	194	1,000	86	52	36	108	62	92
No. errors expected:					163	121	53	179	115	108
H(*ij*):					.47	.57	.32	.40	.46	.15

The number of errors expected in the cumulative scale for item pair AB was calculated as $(1{,}000 - 726)*.596 = 163.30$.
H(AB) was calculated as $1 - 86/163 = 0.47$.

Item coefficients for the cumulative scale:

$E(o)A$: $86 + 52 + 36 = 174$ $E(e)A$: $163 + 121 + 53 = 337$
$H(A) = 1 - 174/337 = .48$

$E(o)B$: $86 + 108 + 62 = 256$ $E(e)B$: $163 + 179 + 115 = 457$
$H(B) = 1 - 256/457 = .44$

> E(o)C: 52 + 108 + 92 = 252   E(e)C: 121 + 179 + 115 = 408
> H(C) = 1 − 252/408 = .38
>
> E(o)D: 36 + 62 + 92 = 190   E(e)D: 53 + 115 + 108 = 276
> H(D) = 1 − 190/276 = .31
>
>   ------   ------
>
> Total Err(obs) =   872 Total Err(exp) =   1,478
>
> $H_{(scale)}$= 1 − 872/1,478 = .41
>
> For total Err(obs) and Err(exp) we can divide by 2, because each pair contributes twice to a model violation.

Table 3.6 A small numerical example for the cumulative scale.

For scales larger than two items, we can inspect not only whether all $H(ij)$s are significantly higher than 0 but also whether all $H(i)$s and the overall **H** are significantly higher than 0 (See Appendix 1 for elaboration).

The use of 0.30 as a lower boundary for the homogeneity of each item and of the scale as a whole is generally far higher than the boundary for statistical significance. A homogeneity value of 0.30 could be insignificant only if the number of respondents is very small (say, below 50), the number of items is very small (say, 2 or 3), and the difficulty of the items is extreme (say, above 0.90 or below 0.10). In analyses where these conditions do not hold, this precaution of testing against the null hypothesis is generally not necessary. We want to keep the lower boundary higher than the boundary for statistical significance for reasons of interpretability or substantive relevance. In our experience scales or items with homogeneity values below 0.30 are difficult to interpret.

3.7 The "Cause" of Errors: Items or Subjects?

When a set of responses to items by subjects does not conform to a perfect Guttman scale, we have until now followed a procedure in which we "blame" the items: The items are not good enough indicators of the same latent trait. But in Guttman's model, an error is simply a violation of the expected relationship between a subject and a pair of items. So the error could just as well be attributed to subjects who march to a different drummer or for whom the questions mean something different.

If we want a measurement instrument that can be used for different groups of subjects, at different time periods, or in different experimental conditions, then we would rather have a scale in which the items function in the same way for all subjects. If necessary, we may discard the items that function differently and work with the maximal subset of items that are still useful. These items can be considered as still sufficiently prototypical indicators for the latent variable.

It is more difficult to justify discarding subjects and working only with a maximal subset of subjects. In that case the researcher faces the problem of generalizing from the remaining sample to a larger population. Often the initial sample was drawn from a well-determined population with a well-specified procedure. If we now delete a number of subjects who do not fit the scale, the remaining sample may no longer represent the original population well. So it is generally preferable to remove items rather than discarding subjects. Nevertheless, there are occasions when one would like to identify and possibly remove the deviant subjects. Let us look at a method for doing this.

3.8 "Blaming" the Subjects: Transposing the Data Matrix and Calculating Subject Homogeneities

One way of determining which subjects give rise to most model violations is simply to count the number of errors against the Guttman scale in each response pattern. But another way takes advantage of the fact that in a perfect Guttman scale the roles of items and subjects are entirely symmetrical, so they can be reversed. Thus, we can simply transpose the matrix, that is, interchange the rows and the columns, as shown in Table 3.7a and 3.7b. In the case of a perfect Guttman scale (Table 3.7a), we get perfect response patterns regardless of whether we show our data matrix with subjects as rows and items as columns, as is usual, or with subjects as columns and items as rows, In both cases we see a lower triangle of 1s and an upper triangle of 0s.

The symmetry between items and subjects underscores that we can evaluate subjects by their individual subject homogeneity as well. A homogeneity coefficient H^T can be calculated for the whole dataset, for individual subjects $H^T(s)$, and for each pair of subjects $H^T(st)$ for subjects s and t, in the same way as the original homogeneity coefficients. The major difference is that the calculation of item homogeneities generally is done over hundreds of subjects, but the calculation of subject homogeneities only over some 5 to 20 items. This means that the estimates of these subject homogeneities have to be taken with a grain of salt.

Meijer (1994) has shown that the number of Guttman errors is a simple and powerful person-fit statistic and that it compares well with other alternatives, such as the subject homogeneity. But establishing subject homogeneity is also useful for the evaluation of probabilistic models, to which we will turn later in this monograph.

Data matrix					
	A	B	C	D	E
1	0	0	0	0	0
2	1	0	0	0	0
3	1	1	0	0	0
4	1	1	1	0	0
5	1	1	1	1	0
6	1	1	1	1	1

Table 3.7a Perfect Guttman scale with subjects 1–6 as rows and items A–E as columns.

Transposed data matrix					
	6	5	4	3	2	1
E	1	0	0	0	0	0
D	1	1	0	0	0	0
C	1	1	1	0	0	0
B	1	1	1	1	0	0
A	1	1	1	1	1	0

Table 3.7b Perfect Guttman scale with items E–A as rows and subjects 6–1 as columns.

3.9 Using Imperfect Patterns to Measure Subject Scale Values

Can we use response patterns that contain errors for the measurement of a subject? This question can be answered with "yes" if we can still assume that the set of items forms a cumulative scale and that the subject understood the questions in the same way as the other people we have tried to measure. If we can use each response pattern to measure a subject, regardless of the number of errors he makes, how do we obtain this measurement?

Since we do *not* define the number of errors in a response pattern on the basis of the number of changes needed to make the pattern perfect, we cannot assign to him the scale value of the nearest perfect pattern. We have also seen that, for the response pattern ABCD,1101, for example, the nearest perfect pattern cannot be assigned unambiguously; it could be either 2 or 4. We therefore opt for defining *the scale value of a subject* who gives a response pattern that contains errors simply as *the number of items to which he has given the positive response.*[3] So subjects with the response pattern ABCD,1101 get 3 as their scale value.

3.10 Conclusion

In this chapter we have discussed how to evaluate a dataset as a cumulative scale, using Loevinger's coefficients of homogeneity. We have also discussed how to measure subjects and items: subjects by the rank order of their scale scores and items by their order of popularity in the dataset. The next chapter is devoted to the question of how to find subsets of items that form a cumulative scale, if the whole set of all items does not, and whether to discard items or subjects in that case.

---

[3]As Mokken (1971, pp. 140–141) demonstrated, this definition of the manifest scale score of subjects correlates highly with their true latent scale score.

CHAPTER 4.
CONFIRMATION OR EXPLORATION

4.1 Searching for Subsets of Scalable Items

So far we have taken a set of items for granted as a cumulative scale. One might say that we have *tested* whether the set of items formed a scale and that the procedure we used was a *test or confirmatory procedure*. But often, in an empirical situation, we do not know ahead of time whether a set of items forms a cumulative scale or not. It is therefore often desirable to explore whether all or at least a subset of the items conform to the requirements of a cumulative scale. In this section I explain how to search through a pool of items for the maximal possible cumulative scale, that is, the cumulative scale with the largest number of items (see also Jacoby, 1991, pp. 35–37, for discussion). This procedure is called the *search or exploratory procedure*.

The procedure for finding the maximal possible scale has two steps. First we find the best possible smallest scale. We could define the smallest scale on the basis of theory, previous research, literature, or intuitions. More commonly, however, we use a standard procedure to select the best smallest scale for us. As the second step, we add the next most scalable item to the existing scale. We continue adding new items to the existing scale one by one as long as they meet the criteria for scalability.

This procedure can be regarded as a hierarchical agglomerative (or bottom-up) clustering procedure. This procedure for item selection stands in contrast to the top-down procedures used in most other models, such as reliability analysis, factor analysis, or parametric IRT models, in which bad items are deleted from the whole scale or the whole factor or test.

The best possible smallest cumulative scale consists of two items. If we have two items, then it is possible to *falsify* that these two items form a scale. We establish the scalability of two items on the basis of the following criteria:

1. The $H(ij)$ coefficient should be significantly higher than 0, that is, $Z(ij) > 1.64$ (one-sided test with an exceedance probability $\alpha = 0.05$), as discussed earlier (see Appendix 2). This implies that the two items are positively correlated.

2. The $H(ij)$ coefficient should be higher than a user-specified lower boundary, usually set to 0.30.

These two criteria are not the same: The first can be regarded as a statistical significance criterion, and the second can be regarded as a substantive relevance criterion. The **H** coefficient can be significantly larger than 0, especially if the sample of subjects is large, but it may nevertheless be very small in absolute size. The second criterion tries to remedy this problem by setting an absolute lower boundary for the coefficient of scalability, such as 0.30.

3. Among all item pairs that conform to the first two criteria, select the item pair with the highest **H**(ij) coefficient.

4. If two or more item pairs are tied for the highest **H**(ij) coefficient, select the pair that contains the least popular item(s). This is an arbitrary criterion to ensure that a unique item pair is always selected.

5. If there are still multiple item pairs that conform to these requirements, take the pair that contains the item(s) that is (are) described first in the dataset. This—finally—ensures a unique best smallest scale.

The smallest scale—or any scale, for that matter—can now be investigated for extension with additional items. This is done in a stepwise manner, in which only one item is added at each step. The best item to add is the one that best satisfies the following conditions:

1. All item pairs consisting of the best next item and one of the items already in the scale must have a positive **H**(ij) coefficient. If even one of all possible **H**(ij) coefficients is slightly negative, that item will be rejected as part of the scale that is being formed. This requirement implies that all items in a scale must be positively correlated.

2. The **H**(i) coefficient of the new item must be significantly higher than 0, that is, its $Z(i) > 1.64$, or related to a user-specified exceedance probability other than 0.05.

3. The **H**(i) coefficient of the new item must be higher than the user-specified lower boundary (often 0.30).

4. The **H** coefficient of the scale as a whole must be higher than the user-specified lower boundary.

5. If more than one item conforms to the first three requirements, select the item that gives the highest **H** coefficient for the scale as a whole.

6. If more than one item conforms to the first four requirements, select the item that has the highest **H**(i) value among the available candidates.

7. If there still is more than one possibility, select the most difficult item.

Three problems often arise in this selection process. First, as more and more items are added to a scale, the $H(i)$ value of items added earlier may drop, even to a level that is too low according to the user-specified lower boundary. But the computer programs with which these analyses are generally done do not (yet) signal this problem. One solution could have been to block a new item from entering the scale if this would cause the $H(i)$ value of an existing item to drop too far. But this solution is not recommended because it places an unwarranted emphasis on the earlier items in the scale. So the user must check all the individual $H(i)$ values of the items in the final scale to establish that each item is still sufficiently homogeneous in the scale. If an item has dropped below the lower boundary, it may need to be discarded.

A second potential problem is known as capitalizing on chance. An item might seem like a good candidate to an existing scale by sheer chance, that is, it accidentally had $H(ij)$ values with the existing items in the scale higher than 0. To minimize this problem, we need to make it more difficult to add a new item. We want to safeguard against capitalizing on chance. A procedure that subsequently lowers the exceedance probability when a new item is added, that initially was set by the researcher (e.g., 0.05), is described in Appendix 2.

The third potential problem is that the best possible scale may be a combination of items that is not found by the procedure just described. Each item is selected as the best possible addition to the existing scale, but the procedure proposed here does not inspect all possible subsets of items as a potential best scale. In the software that was designed to perform this ordinal cumulative scale analysis, it is therefore possible for the user to specify other combinations of items, either as a start set to be extended or as a potential final scale. In practice this option is underused.

4.2 Items Not in the Scale: Rejection and Exclusion

One strict requirement of this search procedure is that all item pairs must be positively correlated, that is, have a positive $H(ij)$ value. This means that as soon as some items are added to a scale, any items that are negatively correlated with them can no longer become part of the same scale. At each step in the clustering procedure we must therefore check whether any items in the scale have a negative $H(ij)$ value with any items still outside the scale. Items outside the scale with a negative homogeneity with items inside the scale will then be *rejected*.

This procedure, taken strictly, may lead to rejection of an item because of one slightly negative $H(ij)$ value, such as –0.01, even though all its other

$H(ij)$ values and its $H(i)$ value are high. It will then be up to the researcher's judgment whether to discard the item or to bring it into the scaling procedure as part of either the start set or the test (rather than search) procedure. The researcher's judgment may tend toward either a more principled (reject item) or a more pragmatic (include item) decision.

Sometimes items should not be allowed into the scale even though all their homogeneity values are positive. This situation arises when the $H(ij)$ values, and consequently the $H(i)$ values, are too low (in general, lower than 0.30). Such items are said to be *excluded* from the scale.

A particular latent variable may sometimes be better understood in terms of two or .more related concepts that do not form one single cumulative scale. For instance, the General Health Questionnaire with 28 items (GHQ-28) forms a weak cumulative scale, but it consists of four stronger subscales that distinguish between substantively important aspects of health, such as psychological and somatic subscales. The search procedure may be used on a large set of items, to explore which items belong in the same cumulative scale. Items that are rejected or excluded from the first scale may then be investigated to see whether they form a second scale. This procedure may be repeated until no further scales are found. Often such a procedure leads to a single large scale with many items, plus a number of remaining small distinct scales. These small scales are often very useful in giving information about aspects of the latent trait under study that are not well covered by the large scale. We recommend starting a new clustering procedure with these remaining scales, which may well turn out to be kernels of separate latent variables. If these small scales are used as start sets, items that already were part of the first scale can turn out to be better represented in one of the other scales. This procedure is known as *search extended.*[1]

---

[1]We may think of this procedure in analogy to factor analysis. The first unrotated factor is regarded as the best combination of all items to measure a single latent trait, but after rotation we may use the same items to measure specific aspects of the latent trait under study.

CHAPTER 5. AN EXAMPLE OF
A CUMULATIVE SCALE

American Religious Beliefs

The American dataset of the World Values Study 2002 contains five questions about Christian religious beliefs: "Do you believe . . . 1. . . . in hell; 2. . . . in life after death; 3. . . . in heaven; 4. . . . that people have a soul; 5. . . . in God."[1] We want to know whether these five questions are all good indicators for a single cumulative scale that measures degree of religious belief. The five questions differ in the number of subjects who give the positive response ("yes") to them. As for other nationalities in the World Values Study 2002, there are more Americans who believe in heaven than in hell. But are these questions related, or do they mean different things to different people? If these questions are related, then believing in hell would imply also believing in heaven, or vice versa. But is this really the case? The questions and the answers based on the unweighted dataset are given in Table 5.1. The questions are ordered on the basis of the percentage of respondents who answered affirmatively. "Do you believe in hell?" is the most difficult item, to which the fewest positive responses were given, and "Do you believe in God?" is the easiest. If the five items form a cumulative scale, it will be in this order.

Do you believe	Yes	No	Don't know
in hell	858 (71.5%)	286 (23.8%)	56 (4.7%)
in life after death	909 (75.8%)	207 (17.2%)	84 (7.0%)
in heaven	1,018 (84.8%)	138 (11.5%)	44 (3.7%)
that people have a soul	1,129 (94.1%)	48 (4.0%)	23 (1.9%)
in God	1,133 (94.4%)	48 (4.0%)	19 (1.6%)

Table 5.1 Answers (in percentages) to five religious questions ($N = 1,200$).

[1]This dataset is available through the major data archives, such as the (American) Inter-University Consortium for Political and Social Research or (the German) GESIS-Leibnitz-Institut für Sozialwissenschaften. It allows the reader to follow the examples in this book and check all calculations by hand.

5.1 Finding the Relevant Elementary Information

First let us dichotomize these data, considering "don't know" to be a negative response.[2] With five items we have $5(5 - 1)/2 = 10$ cross tables. For each cross table we can calculate how many respondents violated the cumulative model (Err(obs)), how many respondents would have violated it if the two items had been statistically unrelated (Err(exp)), and the coefficient of homogeneity for this pair of items. This will be illustrated for Table 5.2 with a numerical explanation. The item "life after death" will be abbreviated as "Life," and the item "belief in Hell" as "Hell."

	0	1	Total
0	157	*134*	291
1	185	724	909
Total	342	858	1,200
Err(Obs) = 134	Err(Exp) = 208.1		**H** = 0.36

Table 5.2 Life (horizontal) by Hell (vertical).

Explanation for this cross table: 909 respondents give the positive response ($1 = yes$) to the item Life, and 858 respondents give the positive response to the item Hell. Item Hell is therefore less popular and more difficult than item Life. A model violation is committed by people who give the positive response to the more difficult item (item Hell) and the negative response to the easier item (item Life). There are 134 such respondents, so Err(Obs) = 134. This cell value is given in italics. If the two items (Hell and Life) were statistically unrelated, then we would expect $(291 * 858)/1,200 = 208.1$ respondents in cell (0,1) of the cross table. So Err(Exp) = 208.1. The coefficient of homogeneity for this pair of items is $\mathbf{H} = 1 - \text{Err(Obs)}/\text{Err(Exp)}$, or $\mathbf{H}(\text{Hell},$ Life$) = 1 - 134/208.1 = 1 - 0.64 = 0.36$.

For this cross table we specified the row item as the easier item and the column item as the more difficult one. In this case will we find the number of model violations in the right-top (0,1) cell of each cross table. If the row

---

[2]We will not deal with problems of missing data in this monograph, other than to stipulate that missing data can be regarded as "not defined as the positive response" and hence as the negative response, or that respondents with any missing data may be listwise deleted. For more information about the imputation of missing values in a Mokken scale, see Huisman (1998, 2000).

item is more difficult than the column item, the number of model violations is found in bottom-left cell (1,0).

5.2 Summarizing the Necessary Elementary Information

The information that is necessary for determining model fit—(Err(obs), Err(exp), and $\mathbf{H}(ij)$—can be summarized in three half matrices, or lower triangles, as shown in Tables 5.3 and 5.4:

	Hell	Life	Heaven	Soul	God
Hell		208.1	130.1	50.8	47.9
Life	134		137.9	53.8	50.8
Heaven	5	66		60.2	56.8
Soul	7	11	17		63.0
God	6	19	8	38	

Table 5.3 Number of model violations observed in each item pair in the lower triangle and number of model violations expected in the upper triangle.

	Hell	Life	Heaven	Soul	God
Hell					
Life	0.36				
Heaven	0.96	0.52			
Soul	0.86	0.80	0.72		
God	0.87	0.63	0.86	0.40	

Table 5.4 Coefficient of homogeneity for each item pair.

5.3 Calculating the Homogeneity of Individual Items and of the Scale as a Whole

On the basis of the pairwise information, we calculate the homogeneity of each item as $\mathbf{H}(i) = 1 - \text{Err(obs)}/\text{Err(exp)}$, where Err(obs) and Err(exp) are defined as the sum of the errors observed and expected, respectively, across the item pairs that contain the item.

Err(Obs)		Err(Exp)	H(i)
Hell	134 + 5 + 7 + 6 = 152	208.1 + 130.1 + 50.8 + 47.9 = 436.9	0.65
Life	134 + 66 + 11 + 19 = 230	208.1 + 137.9 + 53.8 + 50.8 = 450.6	0.49
Heaven	5 + 66 + 17 + 8 = 96	130.1 + 137.9 + 60.2 + 56.8 = 385.0	0.75
Soul	7 + 11 + 17 + 38 = 73	50.8 + 53.8 + 60.2 + 63.0 = 227.8	0.68
God	6 + 19 + 8 + 38 = 71	47.9 + 50.8 + 56.8 + 63.0 = 218.5	0.68

In the same way we now calculate the homogeneity of the scale as a whole.

Total scale: Err(Obs)	Err(exp)
152 + 230 + 96 + 73 + 71 = 622	436.9 + 450.6 + 385.0 +227.8 + 218.5 = 1,718.8
H = 1 –622/1,718.8 = 0.64	

Note that here we use twice the number of errors observed and expected. Dividing both the numbers of errors observed and number of errors expected by 2 does not change the outcome.

5.4 Testing Statistical Significance Against the Null Hypothesis

A scale with an **H** value of 0.64 fits the cumulative model well. But we may still wonder what the probability is that this scale could have been obtained from data that are completely statistically independent (cf. Appendix 1). We use the $Z(ij)$ value for a pair of items, $Z(i)$ for individual items, and Z and for the scale as a whole. Because the test of whether the items form a scale is one-sided (we compare **H** > 0 to **H** ≤ 0 [one-sided] rather than **H** = 0 to **H** ≠ 0 [two-sided]) we can specify a one-sided level such as 5% for alpha (which gives a z value of 1.64), 2.5% ($z = 1.96$), 1% ($z = 2.33$), or 0.1% ($z = 3.10$).

Because all $Z(ij)$ values are higher than 3 (Table 5.5), the homogeneity of all 10 item pairs is clearly statistically significant. We can also calculate the $Z(i)$ values of each of the five items separately: $Z_{\text{Hell}} = 28.07$, $Z_{\text{Life}} = 22.36$,

$Z_{Heaven} = 33.02$, $Z_{Soul} = 25.10$, and $Z_{God} = 24.52$. Finally, we can also calculate the Z value of the scale as a whole: $Z = 41.39$. All the $Z(i)$ values and the Z for the scale as a whole are highly significant.

	Hell	Life	Heaven	Soul	God
Hell					
Life	11.05				
Heaven	22.30	13.49			
Soul	11.86	12.21	14.74		
God	11.67	9.31	17.11	13.34	

Table 5.5 $Z(ij)$: Test against the null model of statistical independence.

The logic behind this procedure is clear, but its practical usefulness is limited. Even when alpha is adjusted from 0.05 to 0.0031, the critical Z value increases to (only) 2.73, whereas the $Z(i)$s increase to over 20, and Z is over 40, so the $H(i)$s and H are supersignificant.

5.5 Using the Pairwise Information to Search for the Best Scale

Given that all $H(ij)$s are well above 0.30, it does not come as a surprise that all five items together form an acceptable cumulative scale. But this is by no means always the case. Often the pairwise homogeneities of items that could plausibly form a scale are not all larger than 0.30, or there is no *a priori* reason to expect that all the available items will be useful indicators of a single latent variable. In such a situation the researcher may want to use scale analysis as a form of hierarchical bottom-up cluster analysis, in which the homogeneity coefficient is used as the coefficient of similarity.

This procedure was introduced and explained in chapter 4. Here we illustrate it briefly using the five items in this example. First, the best item pair is selected: the pair (Hell, Heaven), with $H(ij) = 0.96$. The third item to be added is God, which has the highest $H(ij)$s with Hell and Heaven. The fourth item is Soul, and the fifth and final item is Life. A concise overview of the search procedure is given in Table 5.6.

Item	Mean	Step 1		Step 2		Step 3		Step 4	
		H(i)	Z(i)	H(i)	Z(i)	H(i)	Z(i)	H(i)	Z(i)
Hell	0.72	0.96	22.30	0.94	25.07	0.92	27.68	0.65	28.07
Heaven	0.85	0.96	22.30	0.93	27.63	0.88	31.27	0.75	33.02
God	0.94			0.87	19.78	0.69	23.36	0.68	24.52
Soul	0.94					0.64	22.08	0.68	25.10
Life	0.76							0.49	22.36
Scale		0.96	22.30	0.92	29.78	0.80	37.06	0.64	41.39
Rejected items		None		None		None		None	

Table 5.6 Summary of search procedure.

5.6 Using the Transposed Dichotomous Data Matrix

Just as items to which all subjects give the same response cannot be used to determine homogeneity, subjects who give the same response to all items cannot be used in a homogeneity analysis of the transposed data matrix. In the example of American religious beliefs, more than 70% of the respondents believe in hell, which is the most difficult item. A positive response to all five items was given by 716 subjects (60%), and a negative response to all items was given by 28 subjects (2%). A homogeneity coefficient for the whole scale could be calculated only on the basis of the remaining 456 subjects. The result is given in Table 5.7. H^T was a satisfactory 0.47, and only 2.6% had a negative subject homogeneity $H^T(s)$. As a rule we will accept that the dataset is scalable if the percentage of negative subject homogeneity coefficients is lower than 10%.

Subjects with indiscriminate response patterns are not included in the determination of homogeneity, but if the items form a scale, these subjects can still get a scale value. Subjects who give the negative response to all items get the lowest scale value (0), and subjects who give the positive response to all (k) items get the highest scale value (k).

5.7 Using the Parameters in Our Newly Found Scale

Now that we have found that the five items form a scale, the next question is, "What can we do with this information?" Every statistical model, including every measurement model, is evaluated on the basis of two criteria.

	$\mathbf{H}^T$ for entire group = 0.47;	number of negative $\mathbf{H}^T(s)$ values = 12 (2 + 2 + 2 + 5 + 1) percentage of negative $\mathbf{H}^T(s)$ values = 2.6;	456 observations remain
$\mathbf{H}^T(s)$ distribution			O depicts up to 15 people
Freqs.		$\mathbf{H}^T(s)$ range	
		< <=	
		0.9 1.0	|
46		0.8 0.9	|OOOO
74		0.7 0.8	|OOOOO
		0.6 0.7	|
114		0.5 0.6	|OOOOOOOO
59		0.4 0.5	|OOOO
129		0.3 0.4	|OOOOOOOOO
1		0.2 0.3	|O
		0.1 0.2	|
21		0.0 0.1	|OO
2		−0.1 0.0	|O
2		−0.2 −0.1	|O
		−0.3 −0.2	|
2		−0.4 −0.3	|O
5		−0.5 −0.4	|O
		−0.6 −0.5	|
		−0.7 −0.6	|
1		−0.8 −0.7	|O
		−0.9 −0.8	|
			|
28		extreme 0	|OO
716		extreme 1	|OOOOOOOOOOOOOOOOOOOO OOOOOOOOOOOOOOOO OOOOOOOOOOOOOO

Table 5.7 Homogeneity of the transposed data matrix plus subject homogeneities.

First, does the model fit the data that we analyze? And second, what are the parameters, and how do we interpret them? Our discussion about homogeneity was a discussion about model fit. We will continue that discussion with more tests of model fit in the next chapter, but the results of the homogeneity analysis suggest that our data fit the ordinal IRT model.

So what about the parameters? Because our model is an ordinal model, the parameters are rank orders: a rank order of items and a rank order of subjects. The rank order of items will not come as a surprise: It is the rank order of decreasing popularity (or easiness) of the items, which is generally indicated by the popularity of the items in our sample. The rank order of the subjects is their rank order on the basis of the sum score of the five items. This information is given in Table 5.8. Because the parameters found in this model are not measured at interval level, this model has sometimes been called nonparametric. This term is confusing because parameters *are* estimated. *Nonmetric* and *ordinal* are therefore better descriptions of this model.

The median of this distribution is 5, the mean is 4.2, and the standard deviation is 1.2. According to a *t* test, women have a slightly higher mean value on the scale of religious belief (4.3) than men (4.1), which is statistically significant. Unsurprisingly, when we compare subjects on the basis of their answer to the question "How much confidence do you have in the church?," it turns out that people with a great deal of confidence or quite a lot of confidence have significantly higher mean values (4.6 and 4.4, respectively) on the scale than people with not very much confidence (3.5), which in turn is significantly higher than the mean scale value of the (small number of) people who have no confidence at all in the church (2.8). Note that we use the scale values here as if they were measured not as rank orders but as interval-level measurements. The justification for this interpretation is taken up in chapter 9.

Score	Frequency	Percentage
0	28	2
1	39	3
2	71	6
3	98	8
4	248	21
5	716	60
	1,200	100%

Table 5.8 Scale scores of the scale of religious belief.

5.8 Conclusion

In this chapter we gave an elaborate example of the scalability of five items that measure religious beliefs of Americans in the World Values Study. All items could be included in the scale: Both positive and negative responses were given to each item, and all item homogeneity coefficients were statistically significant and high enough for substantive interpretation. Less than 40% of the subjects gave a response pattern in which some items got a positive and others a negative response. Among these subjects, only a small proportion had a negative subject homogeneity. The measurement values of subjects can be used in further analyses.

The emphasis in this and previous chapters has been on interpreting deviations from the perfect response patterns that form a Guttman scale. Psychometricians have called the emphasis on the coefficient of homogeneity testing a deterministic model with an error theory. In modern IRT the emphasis shifts from deterministic to probabilistic models, in which the categorical distinction between correct and incorrect responses gives way to interpreting each response in a probabilistic manner. It is to such probabilistic models that we turn in the next chapter.

CHAPTER 6. THE PROBABILISTIC DOMINANCE MODEL

Monotone Homogeneity

6.1 Imperfect or Probabilistic Responses?

Let us go back to the deterministic cumulative scaling model of chapter 2. In a deterministic scale a person who gives the positive response to a difficult item also gives the positive response to all the easier items. In such a scale, no errors or model violations occur. But if we allow a certain number of errors, as we did in chapters 3–5, even if we keep them below some upper boundary, we have redefined the model; it is not deterministic anymore. What is it, then?

Because there are so many—often unknown—influences on our response behavior, it is generally too much to expect that only perfect Guttman-type response patterns appear in the answers of subjects to questions. In this chapter we settle for a more modest account. We no longer expect that subjects with a particular scale value (θ_s) will always give the positive response to items with a lower scale value $(\delta_i < \theta_s)$ but only that subjects with a higher scale value will have a higher—or at least not lower—probability of giving the positive response to an item. So we shift our terminology: We do not talk about "errors" or "model violations" anymore; we will talk only about "response tendencies" and "response probabilities." Each response pattern is possible, and has a certain probability of occurring, without implying that it may contain one or more errors.

The deterministic cumulative scaling model can also be formulated in terms of probabilities: The probability of a positive response is zero if $\delta_i > \theta_s$, but it steps up to 1 if $\delta_i \leq \theta_s$ (Figure 6.1). This probability function is called an item response function (IRF).[1] In the deterministic model, the IRFs are called step functions, because the probability of the positive response steps up from 0 to 1 without taking on any intermediate values. In a deterministic scale the IRFs of the different items differ only in the location of the item scale value δ_i.

When there are response patterns that violate the *deterministic* model, these probabilities are clearly no longer 0 and 1 but can be anything in between. As a more lenient criterion for a cumulative scale, we can require the probability of a positive response to an item to increase (or at least not to decrease) as the person's ability increases, as shown in Figure 6.2. In this

---

[1]Older literature refers to IRFs as "item characteristic curves" or "trace lines."

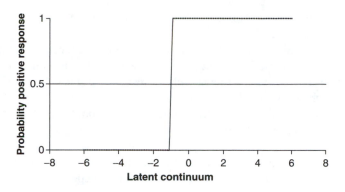

Figure 6.1 Guttman scale: Items are function.

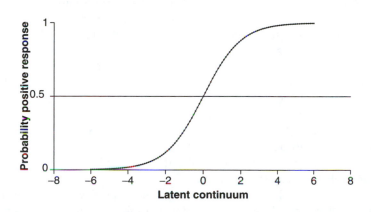

Figure 6.2 Probabilistic Item Response Function.

probabilistic model, the IRFs will look more like *S*-shaped curves (e.g., like logistic functions).

Increasing IRFs. A minimal requirement of the probabilistic cumulative scaling model is that IRFs do not decrease with increasing subject scale value. That is, a subject with a certain value on the latent dimension should have a probability of responding positively to item **i** that is least as high as every subject with a lower value on that latent dimension (e.g., is less

48

able). An item that conforms to this requirement is called a *monotonely homogeneous item.*

In the deterministic model, the scale value of the item can be defined as the particular value on the latent continuum where subjects with scale value θ_s change from responding negatively to responding positively, so $\delta_i = \theta_s$. In the probabilistic model we will define the scale value of the item as identical to the scale value of that subject **s**, for whom the probability of a positive response is exactly 0.50.

Local stochastic independence. A second requirement, which has been implicit so far, is that a person's response to an item depends on his value on the latent trait that we intend to measure, and on nothing else. In a probabilistic model each person has a certain probability of giving the positive response to a given item, depending on his position on the scale, but there are no other systematic influences on whether he gives the positive response.

Consider how a person responds to two items. If his probability of giving the positive response to each of the two items depends only on his scale value, then his probability of giving the positive response to both items is the product of the two separate probabilities. For example, if person A's probability of giving the positive response to item **i** is 0.3 and to item **j** is 0.4, his probability of giving the positive response to both items is 0.3 * 0.4 = 0.12. Person B, who has a slightly higher scale value than person A, has probabilities of giving the positive response to items **i** and **j** of 0.5 and 0.6, so his probability of giving the positive response to both items is 0.5 * 0.6 = 0.30.

The requirement that the probability of giving the positive response to an item depends only on a person's scale value on the latent trait is called *local stochastic independence.* The probabilistic cumulative scaling model assumes that this requirement is met.

To summarize, the probabilistic dominance model can be defined in terms of three model assumptions, similar to the ones mentioned for the deterministic model in chapter 2:

1. The trait to be measured is a single trait and can be represented as a unidimensional continuum.

2. The probability of giving the positive response to each item does not decrease for subjects with increasing values on the latent trait.

3. The probability of giving the positive response to each item depends only on the value of the subject on the latent trait and not on any other systematic influence (i.e., the assumption of local stochastic independence).

6.2 Two Probabilistic Models:
Monotone Homogeneity and Double Monotonicity

When a cumulative scale conforms to the three assumptions just listed, it is possible to order subjects along the latent continuum, that is, to measure them ordinally on a latent trait. This model is known as the monotone homogeneity (MH) model, or the single monotonicity model. It is the first of two models that were formulated by Mokken.

In a second, more restricted model, Mokken added the assumption that the *order* of the probabilities of the positive response to all items is the same for all subjects, regardless of their value on the latent trait. So, every subject **s** should have a probability of responding positively to an item with a certain value on the latent dimension that is higher than (or at least as high as) the probability of responding positively to items with higher scale values, since items with higher values are more difficult and hence less popular. This more restricted model is known as the double monotonicity (DM) model, because not only do the probabilities in the IRFs of each item increase monotonically for subjects with increasing scale values (i.e., from left to right in Figure 6.3), but for each subject they also decrease monotonically for items with increasing scale values (i.e., from top to bottom in Figure 6.3).

This assumption means that all subjects, independent of their scale value, agree about the order of difficulty of the items. If the IRFs do not cross each other, then the order of item difficulties is probabilistically the same for all subjects. In Figure 6.4 this requirement is violated: item C is the most difficult for subjects with $\theta < 0.5$ (where the IRF of item C intersects with the

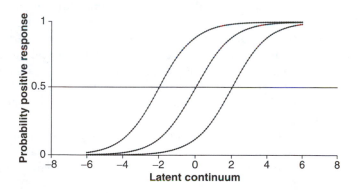

Figure 6.3 Three doubly monotone items.

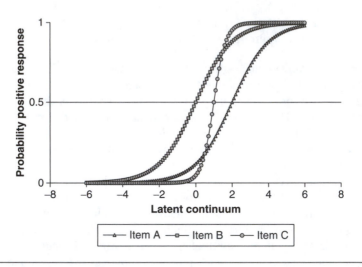

Figure 6.4 Three items, not doubly monotonous.

IRF of item B), it is of intermediate difficulty for subjects with $0.5 < \theta < 1.5$ (where the IRF of item C intersects with the IRF of item A), and it is the easiest for subjects with $\theta > 1.5$.

The importance of the DM model can be understood in the following way. We have tested the homogeneity of a scale and its items in the imperfect cumulative scaling model of chapter 3 by defining a model violation in terms of violating a transitivity relation. In order to use the number of model violations to test a candidate scale, we have to know the order of difficulty of the items. Only if all people agree on the difficulty order of the items can we make an aggregate statement about who responds positively to the difficult item but negatively to the easy item in a particular pair. If the concepts of easy and difficult items mean different things to different people, then it is impossible to set up a cross table for each item pair and identify the error cell. We therefore start out by assuming that the order of difficulty of the items is the same for all people, and we later test this assumption.

So if we compare the IRFs of different items, they should look as in Figure 6.3 and not as it Figure 6.4: If an item has a higher probability of a positive response for one person, then it should have a higher probability of a positive response for all people, irrespective of their level of ability. In other words, IRFs should never cross each other.

6.3 Testing the Model of Monotone Homogeneity

Here I will describe a test of the MH model for one item—say, item **k**—in a set of n dichotomous (0,1) scalable items that violates MH to some degree. We can reconstruct the IRF of this item **k** empirically, using the information we have from the other $(n - 1)$ items of the scale, and test whether the probability of the positive response to this item goes up (or at least does not go down) for subjects with higher scale values.

The scale values of subjects will be based on the sum scores of the remaining $n - 1$ items and so can be between 0 and $n - 1$. Subjects with the same sum score all fall in the same score group. Such a group is called a restscore group, because the scale score is determined on the basis of the remaining (rest of the) items. If item **k** conforms to the requirement of MH, then the proportion of positive responses to item **k** will be higher for subjects in higher restscore groups. This principle will be illustrated with the following example.

In this example we have seven items, with two response categories (0,1) each, that form a cumulative scale. Only one item, item **k**, has a low **H**(i) coefficient of 0.20, and it is this item that violates the model requirement of MH (see Figure 6.5).

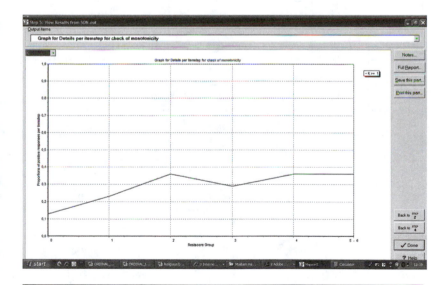

Figure 6.5 Graph of restscore groups (between scores 0 and 5–6) and proportion of positive response to item **k**. One violation (between scores 2 and 3).

Every subject responds to item **k** and to each of the other items. The responses to item **k** in each restscore group (with different sum scores over the other items) are given in Table 6.1. Note that the seven items are unpopular, such that most respondents give the value 0 to all items. The highest score, 7, is given by only 36 subjects. We may consider this as a small group on its own, or we may merge this group with the previous one, to form a new group 6A that is larger.

The proportion of positive responses to item **k** by subjects from different restscore groups increases from 0.13 (505/3,885) for restscore group 1 to 0.23 (244/1,054) for subgroup 2, to 0.36 for subgroup 3, and then it decreases to 0.29 for subgroup 4. It then increases again to 0.36 for group 5, decreases for group 6 to 0.34 and increases again to 0.44 for subgroup 7.

If the last two groups are merged into group 6A, its proportion of positive response is also 0.36. Since it is advisable to make restscore groups of at least 50 subjects, such that each subject does not count for more than 2% of the group, we will ignore the decrease in proportion between groups 5

Restscore group						
Low	*High*	*N*	*Frequencies per item value*		*Mean*	*Proportions of positive responses per item step*
			0	1		≥1
1	0	3,885	3,380	505	0.13	0.13
2	1	1,054	810	244	0.23	0.23
3	2	840	538	302	0.36	0.36
4	3	838	591	247	0.29	0.29
5	4	253	162	91	0.36	0.36
6	5	163	107	56	0.34	0.34
7	6	36	20	16	0.44	0.44
[6A	5 and 6	199	127	72	0.36	0.36]

Table 6.1 Detailed information to determine whether item **k** violates the model of monotone homogeneity.

and 6. A second reason for ignoring this last violation is that its size is only 0.02 (0.36 – 0.34). As a rule, only violations of 0.03 or more will be investigated, but this is a decision for the researcher.

So we will concentrate on the model violation between restscore groups 3 and 4 and assume that we have only six different restscore groups, having merged group 7 and group 6 (see Figure 6.5). How seriously do we need to take this violation of 0.0648 (0.3595 – 0.2947)? Is it possible that this violation can be explained away on the basis of random fluctuations in restscore groups of 840 and 838 subjects?

In Table 6.2 the decrease from 302/840 = 0.3595 to 247/838 = 0.2947 in the 2×2 table would be due to sampling variation if the two population fractions were equal. The exact probability of exceedance is the probability of finding the value 247 or less for score group 4 and item $\mathbf{k} = 1$ in the hypergeometric distribution with marginals 840, 838, 1,129, and 549 (see Molenaar & Sijtsma, 2000, pp. 71–72).

A good normal approximation to this hypergeometric distribution has the normal deviate $z = 2 \times [\sqrt{(f_{11} + 1)} \times (f_{00} + 1) - \sqrt{(f_{01} \times f_{10})}]/\sqrt{(N + 1)}$, or
$z = 2 \times [\sqrt{(248 \times 539)} - \sqrt{(302 \times 591)}]/\sqrt{1,679} = 2 \times (\sqrt{133,672} - \sqrt{178,482})/40.98$
$= 2 \times (365.61 - 422.47)/40.98 = 2.78$.

At the one-sided significance level of 5%, this z value is higher than the critical value of 1.64. Therefore, this violation is considered to be statistically significant and not due to sampling error.

Is this significant model violation sufficient grounds to discard item $\mathbf{k}$? Molenaar and Sijtsma (2000) devised a criterion, called crit, that takes into account a number of aspects in model violation: the number of items, or rather, the number of comparisons with other items in restscore groups (appropriate comparisons [ac]), the number of violations in these comparisons (#vi), the magnitude of these violations in several forms (such as the maximal violation [maxvi], the sum of the violations [sum], and the

	Item $\mathbf{k} = 0$	Item $\mathbf{k} = 1$	Total
Score group 3	538	302	840
Score group 4	591	247	838
Total	1,129	549	1,678

Table 6.2 Cross table to check whether score group 3 and 4 come from a single population.

number of statistically significant violations [#sig]), and a low $H(i)$ coefficient (lower than 0.30). The formal definition of crit is

$$\text{Crit} = 50[.30 - H(i)] + \sqrt{\#vi} + 100\#vi/\#ac + 100 \text{ maxvi} + 10\sqrt{\text{sum}} +$$
$$1{,}000\text{sum}/\#ac + 5 \text{ zmax} + 10\sqrt{\#sig} + 100\#zsig/ac$$

Model violations are compensated by homogeneity values $H(i)$ larger than 0.30. In this case, the low $H(i)$ value of 0.20 adds to the criterion. The requirement of MH holds for all pairs of restscore groups. So if there are 7 different restscore groups, there are 21 pairs of groups, or appropriate comparisons, and with 6 restscore groups there are only 15. Comparisons with extreme restscore groups that have a probability of positive response of exactly 0 or exactly 1 are considered irrelevant, which means that in such cases the number of appropriate comparisons may even be smaller. If there is only one pair of restscore groups in which a model violation occurs, as is the case in this example, then that violation is the maximum violation and the sum of all violations. The violation was significant, so the (maximal) significant z value is 2.78, and only the one violation is significant (#zsig).

This all leads to a crit value of $50 \times 0.10 + \sqrt{1} + 100 \times 1/15 + 100 \times 0.06 + 10\sqrt{0.06} + 1{,}000 \times 0.06/15 + 5 \times 2.78 + 10\sqrt{1} + 100 \times 1/15 = 5 + 1 + 6.7 + 6 + 2.5 + 4 + 13.9 + 10 + 6.5 = 55.6$.

Molenaar regards crit values below 40 as explainable from random fluctuations and crit values above 80 as serious. This value of crit = 56 falls somewhere in between and warrants further attention of the researcher.

6.4 Testing Monotone Homogeneity of Our Five Religious Belief Items

The empirical test of whether the IRF of each item monotonically increases is given by comparing the subjects on the basis of their sum scores on the remaining items, the restscores. Table 6.3 gives the sum scores of the subjects, based on all five items, as well as five sets of restscores, each based on deleting one of the five items.

For each of the five sets of restscore groups, the frequency of the positive response to the deleted item is given in Table 6.4 as $N(1)$, as well as the proportion of the positive response to the size of the restscore group (p). For item Hell, for instance, group 1: $0/28 = 0.00$; group 2: $2/41 = 0.05$; group 3: $6/75 = 0.08$; group 4: $134/226 = 0.59$; and group 5: $716/830 = 0.86$. Relevant for the test is that the order of the proportions is indeed monotonically increasing: 0.00–0.05–0.08–0.59–0.86. This property of monotonically increasing IRFs is found for all five items (see Table 6.4).

Number of positive responses	All 5 items	Without				
		Hell	Life	Heaven	Soul	God
0	28	28	28	28	46	49
1	39	41	53	48	80	76
2	71	75	117	107	102	106
3	98	226	157	301	254	250
4	248	830	845	716	718	719
5	716					
Total	1,200	1,200	1,200	1,200	1,200	1,200

Table 6.3 Number of respondents in different score groups for all items and different restscore groups after deleting a specific item.

Group number	Restscore	Hell		Life		Heaven		Soul		God	
		$N(1)$	p	$N(1)$	p	$N(1)$	p	$N(1)$	p	$N(1)$	p
1	0	0	0.00	0	0.00	0	0.00	18	0.39	21	0.43
2	1	2	0.05	14	0.26	9	0.19	59	0.74	58	0.76
3	2	6	0.08	60	0.51	45	0.42	90	0.88	93	0.88
4	3	134	0.59	119	0.76	248	0.82	246	0.97	245	0.98
5	4	716	0.86	716	0.85	716	1.00	716	1.00	716	1.00

Table 6.4 Number and proportion of respondents in different restscore groups who gave the positive response to the deleted item.

Because we have five different score groups, we can make $5(5–1)/2 = 10$ different comparisons between score groups (1 vs. 2, 1 vs. 3, . . . 4 vs. 5). For each of these comparisons the lower group should not have a higher proportion than the higher group. However, if the proportion is exactly 0 or exactly 1, then comparisons have become completely predictable: No score group has a proportion lower than 0 or higher than 1. This means that score groups with proportions of exactly 0 or 1 are excluded from these comparisons. So with item Soul and item God all 10 comparisons are still useful, but with the items Hell and Life only six comparisons are still useful, and for item Heaven only three (groups 2 vs. 3, 2 vs. 4, and 3 vs. 4).

In this example we selected a minimum size for each of the restscore groups of 25. In this case all five restscore groups remained distinct. But because some of the restscore groups can be small, we generally want large enough groups. What happens to the test of MH if we increase the size of the restscore groups to consist of at least 120 people? The information from Table 6.3 is now aggregated in Table 6.5. For item Hell the first three score groups need to be combined, to reach a minimum of 120 people. For item God the first two score groups need to be combined, as well as score groups 2 and 3 to reach the 120-person level. Now Table 6.6 can be created to inspect the monotone increase in p values for each of the groups if one of the items is deleted.

					Without					
	Hell		Life		Heaven		Soul		God	
Group	a	b	a	b	a	b	a	b	a	b
1	0–2	144	0–2	198	0–2	183	0–1	126	0–1	125
2	3	226	3	157	3	301	2–3	356	2–3	356
3	4	830	4	845	4	716	4	718	4	719
		1,200		1,200		1,200		1,200		1,200

Table 6.5 Number of respondents in different score groups for all items, and different restscore groups after deleting a specific item (minimum group size: 120 people).

a. Restscore value.

b. Number of respondents with restscore value.

				Deleted item					
	Hell		Life		Heaven		Soul		God	
Group	N(1)	p	N(1)	p	N(1)	p	N(1)	p	N(1)	p
1	8	0.06	74	0.37	54	0.30	77	0.61	79	0.63
2	134	0.59	119	0.76	248	0.82	336	0.94	338	0.95
3	716	0.86	716	0.85	716	1.00	716	1.00	716	1.00

Table 6.6 Number ($N(1)$) and proportion (p) of respondents in different restscore groups who gave the positive response to the deleted item.

With the exception of item Heaven, where only the comparison can be made between groups 1 and 2, with the other items all three comparisons can be made (1 vs. 2, 1 vs. 3, and 2 vs. 3). Note that the p value for group 3 and items Soul and God is approximated and not exactly 1.00 (716/718 and 716/719, respectively). For none of the items was the requirement of MH falsified.

CHAPTER 7. THE PROBABILISTIC DOMINANCE MODEL

Double Monotonicity

7.1 The Importance of Double Monotonicity

It is difficult to overstate the importance of the DM model. Because the measurement scales we use do not have a standard unit of measurement, and because the measurement values we find often depend on the specific group of subjects that are being measured, it is difficult in applied research to compare measurements taken from different cultures, different samples, or different time periods. A measurement scale that conforms to the requirement of the DM model implies that in any population, any sample, any time period, or any experimental condition the ordering of subjects according to their scale value is the same.

We will discuss five different ways of assessing DM. The first way was already described by using the transposed data matrix in chapters 3 and 5. In assessing the homogeneity of the scale, and of the individual subjects, we use one single order of the items for all subjects. If the subject homogeneities are high, we may conclude that there were no substantial model violations in assuming the same order of the items for all subjects. In addition to this test, four different tests for DM will be described: using external groups, the rest-score method, the restsplit method, and the P(+,+) and P(−,−) matrices.

7.2 Testing Double Monotonicity With External Groups

If the order of difficulty or popularity of the items must be the same for all subjects, then the least we can do is to check whether the order is the same for subgroups of subjects who are relevant for our study. These can be subgroups based on demographic variables, such as gender, age, education, or church membership, or on attitudinal variables, such as—for the present example of American religious beliefs—importance of praying or confidence in the church. The choice of group criteria depends on the research context.

In the World Values Study a number of other questions are asked about religion, such as "How important is religion in your life?" and "How much confidence do you have in the church?" In the unweighted American dataset, 454 respondents had a great deal of confidence in the church, 450 had quite a lot of confidence, and the 296 remaining respondents did not have very much confidence, or none at all, or did not say.

We may wonder whether these three groups of respondents differ in how they think about the five items as measuring the latent trait of degree in religious belief. Would the items mean the same thing to members of these three groups? If this is not the case, then it is possible that the order of popularity of the items would differ between groups. And if this is the case, comparing scale values between these three groups might mean that the scale values were based on the positive response to different items. The result of homogeneity analyses for the three groups is given in Table 7.1.

There are differences in the homogeneity values of the items for the three groups. But our first concern now is whether this is still the same scale, that is, one in which the items have the same order of popularity. That is the requirement for DM that we are investigating now. This is not the case: For the "great deal of confidence" group, item Life is now less popular (0.81) than item Hell (0.86), and for the "not much confidence" group, item Soul is more popular (0.85) than item God (0.83) (proportions in italics in Table 7.1).

We could have done an analysis in which the items are ordered according to popularity in their own subgroup. So we reversed the order of item Life and item Hell for the subgroup "A great deal," and we reversed the order of item God and item Soul for the subgroup "Not much or none at all." These reversals in order led to higher homogeneity values (Table 7.2).

| | How much confidence do you have in the church? | | | | | | |
| | Whole dataset | | A great deal | | Quite a lot | | Not much or none at all | |
	$p(i)$	$H(i)$	$p(i)$	$H(i)$	$p(i)$	$H(i)$	$p(i)$	$H(i)$
Hell	0.71	0.65	0.86	0.32	0.72	0.63	0.47	0.75
Life	0.76	0.49	0.81	0.25	0.81	0.48	0.59	0.51
Heaven	0.85	0.75	0.96	0.65	0.89	0.72	0.61	0.71
Soul	0.94	0.68	0.97	0.56	0.97	0.65	0.85	0.65
God	0.94	0.68	0.99	0.50	0.97	0.63	0.83	0.63
N, H	1,200	0.64	454	0.38	450	0.61	296	0.65

Table 7.1 p values and H values for the religious belief scale and items for the whole dataset and for subgroups with different degrees of confidence in the church.

How much confidence do you have in the church?					
A great deal			Not much or none at all		
	$p(i)$	$\mathbf{H}(i)$		$p(i)$	$\mathbf{H}(i)$
Life	*.81*	0.32	Hell	.47	0.75
Hell	*.86*	0.41	Life	.59	0.51
Heaven	.96	0.65	Heaven	.61	0.71
Soul	.97	0.56	*God*	*.83*	0.65
God	.99	0.50	*Soul*	*.85*	0.68
N, **H**	454	0.45		296	0.66

Table 7.2 *p* Values and **H** values for subgroups when items are ordered according to difficulty in their own subgroup.

The difference for the last group ("Not much or none at all") seems negligible, but the difference in homogeneity for the first group is quite substantial.

So how do we test whether the differences in the order of the items can be explained by random variation within a single population? Let us take the example of item Life and item Hell in the subgroup "A great deal" (Table 7.3).

Life is less popular than Hell in this subgroup, because cell (0,1) is higher (63) than cell (1,0) (41). The McNemar test that these differences can be explained from randomness in a single population was proposed by

		Hell		*Total*
Life		0	1	
0		21	63	84 (19%)
1		41	329	370 (81%)
Total		62 (14%)	392 (86%)	454

Table 7.3 Cross table of item Life (vertical) and item Hell (horizontal) in subgroup "A great deal of confidence in the church."

Molenaar (1970, formula 5.5 of chapter 5, p. 100). He used the following general formula:

$$z = \sqrt{(2k + 2 + b)} - \sqrt{(2n - 2k + b)}, \text{ in which}$$
$$b = [(2k + 1 - n)^2 - 10n]/12n$$

In this formula k is the smallest of the two frequencies, 41, and n is the sum of the two frequencies: $41 + 63 = 104$.

$$\text{So } b = [(2 \times 41 + 1 - 104)^2 - 10 \times 104]/$$
$$12 \times 104 = (-21)^2 - 1{,}040/1{,}248 = 441 - 1{,}040/1{,}248 = -0.48$$
$$\text{And } z = \sqrt{(2 \times 41 + 2 - 0.48)} - \sqrt{(2 \times 104 - 2 \times 41 - 0.48)} =$$
$$\sqrt{83.52} - \sqrt{125.52} = 9.139 - 11.204 = 2.065$$

This value is significant, and we will need to take this value seriously.

Whether this will lead us to discard item Life or item Hell from our test will depend on other aspects of model violation as well, as is summarized in the crit value. For item Hell the crit value turns out to be 41, and for item Life crit = 49. In this case we would be willing to accept both items in the scale, even with this significant model violation.

Two additional points should be made when we perform separate scale analyses for different subgroups. First, the popularity of the items may differ substantially between the subgroups. We may well expect that the items of religious belief will be more popular among subjects who have a great deal of confidence in the church than among subjects who don't. This is indeed the case. For a scale analysis that tries to establish whether all items measure the same latent trait, this difference in item popularities is no problem. The fact that the subgroups differ systematically in their scale scores only underscores the validity of the scale. Second, both the scale and the individual items may have different coefficients of homogeneity in different subgroups. This need not be a problem either. It is possible that the 454 respondents who have a great deal of confidence would all be very religious, and would all have the same high scale value. If that were the case, then this group of respondents might be too homogeneous, and under the assumption of local stochastic independence, any differences in their responses would be attributable to random noise. That, in turn, would mean that the number of observed model violations would be close to the number of expected violations, and hence the coefficients of homogeneity would be low.

The coefficient of homogeneity is an adapted correlation coefficient, and the value of a correlation coefficient is known to depend on the variance of items. The more homogeneous a group of subjects, the more the group of points in a scatter plot looks like a circle than like a long cigar, and the more difficult it is to estimate a precise regression line through it. If subjects do not differ very much on some dimension, then it will be difficult to establish differences accurately. This is in fact the extension of the principle of local stochastic independence: If all subjects have exactly the same scale value on the latent dimension, then we will not find a homogeneous scale. So if we want to compare subgroups, we are not very interested in differences in the coefficients of homogeneity.[1]

7.3 Testing Double Monotonicity With Restscore Groups

Is it sufficient to compare the order of the items for different external groups? No. No test is ever enough. This answer stems from Popper's ideas about verification and falsification in science. According to Popper (1959, 1963/2003) one can never know that something is forever true because it is impossible to test every instance. However, it is possible to accept something as temporarily true, as long as there is no evidence to the contrary. It is good scientific reasoning, then, to try to show that severe and stringent tests that may elicit counterevidence do not form a rejection of the (temporary) truth of a statement, such as the acceptance of the requirement of DM of a scale.

There are several other possibilities to assess whether IRFs do not intersect in which we do not make use of external groups. We can use an approach that is very similar to the approach taken when we tested MH. There we looked at the IRF of every item separately for groups with increasing scale values, based on their scores of the remaining $(n-1)$ items. Now we shall look at the difficulty order of every pair of IRFs for subjects with increasing scale scores based on the remaining $(n-2)$ items. With $n-2$ items, we can create at most $n-1$ different groups, with scale values between 0 and $n-2$ (for dichotomous 0,1 responses). Subjects in each of these groups respond to the item pair under scrutiny. Let us call this the item pair $(\mathbf{i},\mathbf{j})$. So in each restscore group all four responses are possible to the item pair $(\mathbf{i},\mathbf{j})$: 00, 01, 10, and 11. If item $\mathbf{j}$ is easier, or more popular, than item $\mathbf{i}$ in the whole sample, then item $\mathbf{j}$ should be more popular than item $\mathbf{i}$ in each restscore group. So in each restscore group, $f(01) + f(11) > f(10) + f(11)$, or, more simply, $f(01) > f(10)$.

---

[1]As a note of historical interest, Mokken (1971) formulated a test that checked whether the coefficients of homogeneity in two samples were the same. He argued that it might be interesting to investigate in a group of subjects whether some indicators of a latent trait would show more homogeneity over time, for instance, in a socialization process. However, there is an alternative interpretation of differences in homogeneity: The less variation in the scale scores there is among the subjects, the more their response patterns are locally stochastically independent. Difference in variation may lead to difference in homogeneity. The fact that it was not possible to distinguish between these different interpretations was the main reason for not using this test anymore.

If this is not the case, then we will use the normal approximation to the binomial distribution to test whether we can accept the hypothesis that in the population $f(01) = f(10)$. In order to do this, we follow the same McNemar test that was used earlier in the inspection of a violation of DM in external groups.

We can apply that test to our substantive example of American religious beliefs. We will first begin with a comparison on the basis of restscore groups based on three of the five items. The size of these restscore groups obviously depends on which pair of items are deleted. The sizes are given in Table 7.4.

As it turns out, in only one of the 10 sets of restscore groups—namely the restscore groups found when the items Life and Heaven are deleted—do we find a slight sign of lack of DM (Figure 7.1). For each of the four restscore groups we can make a cross table of the deleted items (Table 7.5).

	Item pairs deleted									
Restscores	Hell Life	Hell Heaven	Hell Soul	Hell God	Life Heaven	Life Soul	Life God	Heaven Soul	Heaven God	Soul God
0	28	28	46	51	28	58	51	47	57	113
1	58	53	85	77	70	123	142	125	110	111
2	120	239	232	237	256	171	158	309	313	254
3	994	880	837	835	846	848	849	719	720	722

Table 7.4 Number of respondents in restscore groups if two items are deleted.

Group	Score	N	Cross table Life by Heaven				v	z	p Life	p Heaven
			00	01	10	11				
1	0	28	28	0	0	0			0.00	0.00
2	1	70	39	9	14	8	0.07	0.83	0.31	0.24
3	2	256	48	37	52	119	0.06	1.49	0.67	0.61
4	3	846	1	129	0	716			0.85	1.00
Total		1,200	116	175	66	843	0.13		0.76	0.85

Table 7.5 Cross tables of item Life by item Heaven for the four different restscore groups based on the three remaining items.

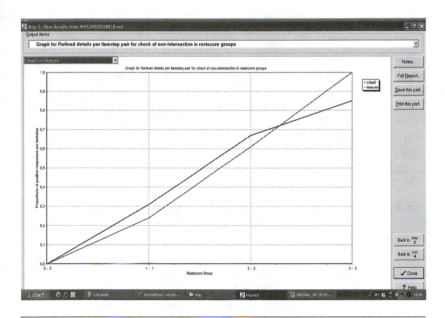

Figure 7.1 Graphical display of lack of DM of item pair Life and Heaven.

The Ns in Table 7.5 are obviously the same as the Ns in Table 7.4, column "Life Heaven." We know that item Heaven is easier and more popular than item Life for the whole population. Therefore, item Heaven must be easier than item Life in each of the four rest groups. In the first restscore group, in which the three remaining items have all been negatively answered (because the sum score is 0), nobody gave a positive response to the two items.

In the last subgroup, in which all three remaining items were answered positively, 716 respondents also responded positively to these last two items. In addition, 129 respondents answered positively to the second item (Heaven) but not to the first (Life) (column 01), but there were no respondents who gave the reverse, (1,0) response. So in total in this group 716 of the 846 respondents gave the positive response to item Life (which is a proportion of 0.85), whereas all 845 (129 + 716) respondents (or a proportion of 1.00) gave the positive response to item Heaven. This higher proportion for item Heaven in this subgroup corresponds to the higher proportion for the whole sample, so this subgroup conforms to the expectation of DM.

However, groups 2 and 3, with restscores 1 and 2, respectively, do not conform to this expectation. In group 2 item Life is more popular ($p = .31$) than item Heaven ($p = .24$). The difference in the wrong direction (v) is $0.31 - 0.24 = 0.07$. And in group 3, Life is also more popular ($p = .67$)

than item Heaven ($p = .61$). The difference in the wrong direction now is $0.67 - 0.61 = 0.06$.

Should we worry about these violations? Or could they perhaps be explained away as random deviations that can easily happen in groups of this size and with these marginal frequency distributions? The answer is given in the test that was explained earlier for external groups, and the relevant z scores are 0.83 and 1.49, respectively. These are both lower than 1.64, the one-sided criterion for an alpha of 5%, so none of these violations are regarded as significant. Moreover, crit (Life) = 37 and crit (Heaven) = 24, which are both below the norm of 40, so we do not need to worry about them.

7.4 Testing Double Monotonicity With Restsplit Groups

A possible problem with the rest group approach is that the groups can be rather small, and therefore the test is not very powerful. In order to improve the power of the test, we can merge the different restscore groups. If there are m restscore groups with scores 0 to $m - 1$, then there are $m - 1$ ways to split them into the lower and the higher groups: (score group 0) versus (score group 1 to score group $m - 1$); (score group 0 and 1) versus (score group 2 to score group $m - 1$) ... (score group 0 to score group $m - 2$) versus (score group $m - 1$). For each of the $m - 1$ possible dichotomizations we can now test the assumption of DM both in the lower and in the higher set of restscore groups.

If we apply this principle to Table 7.4, with four different rest group scores (0 to 3), we can split or dichotomize them in three different ways (Tables 7.6, 7.7, and 7.8). It turns out that in the first dichotomization (Table 7.6) we find no violations of DM. But in the last two dichotomizations (Table 7.7 and 7.8) we do. The first violation is not significant ($z = 0.83$, using the McNemar test used earlier), but the second one ($z = 1.80$) is.

Group	Score	N	Cross table Life by Heaven				v	z	p Life	p Heaven
			00	01	10	11				
1 Low	0–0	28	28	0	0	0			0.00	0.00
2 High	1–3	1,172	88	175	66	843			0.78	0.87
Total		1,200	116	175	66	843			0.76	0.85

Table 7.6 Dichotomization 1: Score groups 0 versus 1–3.

Group	Score	N	Cross table Life by Heaven				v	z	p Life	p Heaven
			00	01	10	11				
1 Low	0–1	98	67	9	14	8	0.05	0.83	0.22	0.17
2 High	2–3	1,102	49	166	52	835			0.80	0.91
Total		1,200	116	175	66	843	0.05		0.76	0.85

Table 7.7 Dichotomization 2: Score groups 0–1 versus 2–3.

Group	Score	N	Cross table Life by Heaven				v	z	p Life	p Heaven
			00	01	10	11				
1 Low	0–2	354	115	46	66	127	0.06	1.80	0.55	0.49
2 High	3–3	846	1	129	0	716			0.85	1.00
Total		1,200	116	175	66	843	0.06		0.76	0.85

Table 7.8 Dichotomization 3: Score groups 0–2 versus 3.

Notice that in both cases it is the lower set of groups that contains the violation, not the higher group.

We can interpret this in terms of the discrimination—the steepness of the item response function—of the items. If the violation exists in the low group, the more difficult item is too easy for respondents with low scale scores but not for respondents with high scale scores. Such an item on the whole has a less steep slope than the other item and discriminates less. If the violation exists in the high group, then the more difficult item is too easy for respondents with high scale scores but not for respondents with low scale scores. Such an item on the whole has a steeper slope than the other item and discriminates more. In this case, it seems that item Life discriminates less than item Heaven.

7.5 Testing Double Monotonicity With the P(+,+) and P(–,–) Matrices

Another way to check whether IRFs do not intersect is by following the logic based on the assumption of local stochastic independence. Given three items, **i**, **j**, and **k**, in order of popularity, $p(i) > p(j) > p(k)$. If the IRFs do not intersect, then this is also true for each subject **s**, with scale value θ_s: $p^s(i) > p^s(j) > p^s(k)$. The assumption of local stochastic independence implies that for each subject **s**, the probability of a response pattern to a series of items is simply the product of the probability of each individual item. So for subject **s** the probability of a positive response to both **i** and **j** can be written as $p^s(ij) = p^s(i) \times p^s(j)$. This implies that, given local stochastic independence, $p^s(ij) > p^s(ik) > p^s(jk)$. Now, if the IRFs do not intersect, then this order is the same for all subjects, so it is true for the whole sample, and we may delete the superscript s: $p(ij) > p(ik) > p(jk)$. This information about positive (+) responses to pairs of items is stored in a square matrix that is called the P(+,+) matrix. When the items in this matrix are ordered from least to most popular, the cell frequencies for each row and for each column should increase from low to high proportions.

The same reasoning can be followed when we focus on the negative (–) response instead: When $1 - p(i) < 1 - p(j) < 1 - p(k)$, or $p(i)^- < p(j)^- < p(k)^-$, then—if local independence holds and the IRFs do not intersect—also $p(i^-j^-) < p(i^-k^-) < p(j^-k^-)$. The information about negative responses to pairs of items is stored in the P(–,–) matrix. When the items in this matrix are ordered from least to most popular, the cell frequencies for each row and each column should decrease from high to low proportions. Here I will prove that if a particular model violation occurs in the P(+,+) matrix, it cannot occur in the P(–,–) matrix and vice versa.

We will show how this procedure works using our substantive example. From Tables 5.1–5.3 we can derive the values of the (1,1) or (+,+) cells, and the values of the (0,0) or (–,–) cells for each of the 10 item pairs. If these are put together in a square symmetrical matrix with the items in their order of decreasing difficulty, the cell values should increase (for the P(+,+) matrix) or decrease (for the P(–,–) matrix) monotonically, both row-wise and column-wise. Rather than using the cell frequencies, we use the proportions, by dividing by the total number of respondents. The relevant information is then given in Tables 7.9, 7.10, and 7.11.

How do we systematically inspect these matrices for model violation? Because the matrices are symmetrical, it does not make a difference whether we inspect them row-wise or column-wise. Let us just say that we inspect them column-wise, and let us begin with the P(+,+) matrix and the columns Hell and Life. Going down these two columns, we compare the cell values for the remaining three items: Heaven, 0.71–0.70; Soul, 0.71–0.75; and God, 0.71–0.74. Because Hell is less popular than Life, for each of these three pairs of numbers the first should not be higher than the second. However, this is the case for row Heaven, because 0.71 > 0.70.

If we concentrate on item Hell, we can combine it with each of the remaining (column) items and then row-wise compare the two cells and

	Hell	Life	Heaven	Soul	God
Hell		157	177	64	61
Life	724		116	60	48
Heaven	853	843		54	59
Soul	851	898	1,001		29
God	852	890	1,010	1,091	

Table 7.9 Information for the P(+,+) and P(−,−) matrix. Lower triangle: frequencies in (1,1) cell; upper triangle: frequencies in the (0,0) cell; $N = 1,200$.

		Hell	Life	Heaven	Soul	God
	p	0.71	0.76	0.85	0.94	0.94
Hell	0.71		0.60	0.71	0.71	0.71
Life	0.76	0.60		0.70	0.75	0.74
Heaven	0.85	0.71	0.70		0.83	0.84
Soul	0.94	0.71	0.75	0.83		0.91
God	0.94	0.71	0.74	0.84	0.91	

Table 7.10 P(+,+) matrix: Symmetrical matrix, derived from the lower triangle of Table 7.9, dividing by $N = 1,200$.

see whether the first cell of the pair is higher than the second. We find no problems with items Life and Heaven but one more problem with item pair Soul–God: in row Life, the cell values are 0.75–0.74.

Because each item is involved with $k − 1 = 4$ other items, and each column pair is involved with $k − 2 = 3$ row items, the total number of appropriate comparisons of each item is $(k − 1)(k − 2) = 12$. This number can become smaller if the first proportion is exactly 0 or the last proportion is exactly 1.00.

Now we do the same for the P(−,−) matrix, in which for each column pair of items the cell values in each row should not increase. Violations are found

		Hell	Life	Heaven	Soul	God
	$1 - p$	0.28	0.24	0.15	0.06	0.06
Hell	0.28		0.13	0.15	0.05	0.05
Life	0.24	0.13		0.10	0.05	0.04
Heaven	0.15	0.15	0.10		0.04	0.05
Soul	0.06	0.05	0.05	0.04		0.02
God	0.06	0.05	0.04	0.05	0.02	

Table 7.11 P(−,−) matrix: Symmetrical matrix, derived from the upper triangle of Table 7.9, dividing by $N = 1,200$.

for column pair (Life, Heaven) with row Hell, 0.13—0.15, and with row God, 0.04—0.05, and for column pair (Soul, God) with row Heaven, 0.04—0.05.

How can we evaluate the model violations in the P(+,+) or P(−,−) matrix? The model violation that we found in the P(−,−) matrix says that whereas the negative response to item Heaven is less popular than the negative response to item Life, the negative response to item pair (Hell, Heaven) is more popular than the negative response to item pair (Hell, Life). So something is wrong when we compare the cross tables of item Heaven by item Life for the different responses to item Hell. For the P(−,−) matrix, we are particularly interested in the negative response to item Hell, because the marginals of that table give us the proportions of negative response to item pairs (Hell, Life) and (Hell, Heaven).

This model violation can be defined by the fact that the (1,0) cell in the left side of Table 7.12 (44) is smaller than the (0,1) cell of that table (64) (the right side of Table 7.12 can be ignored). If these values were the same, then there would be no model violation anymore. The test whether the values 44 and 64 come from a population in which the probabilities of the responses to these two cells are equal is the same (McNemar) test already described for testing violations with external groups. In this case, the value for z is 1.83, which is significant. However, crit(Life) = 31 and crit(Heaven) = 18, so we will not worry about these results. Moreover, because the violation was only 0.02, in the default inspection (where the minimum violation is 0.03) we would have glossed over this violation.

	Hell = 0				Hell = 1		
Heaven → Life ↓	0	1	Total	Heaven → Life ↓	0	1	Total
0	113	64	177	0	3	2	5
1	44	121	165	1	131	722	853
Total	157	185	342		134	724	858

Table 7.12 Heaven (horizontal) by Life (vertical) by Hell (third dimension).

7.6 What Inferences Can We Draw From Tests of the Probabilistic Models?

The tests of the probabilistic models are generally not standalone tests but are almost always performed on a set of items that already have a high enough homogeneity (cf. Mokken, Lewis, & Sijtsma, 1986; Roskam, van den Wollenberg, & Jansen, 1986). They then do not lead to a rejection of the scale as a homogeneous measurement instrument, but they may point to individual items that should be reconsidered for admission in the scale. Which of these tests is most important? Again, I refer to the idea of falsification: *All* tests are important! *Any* significant falsification should concern the researcher. We have no prescriptions for which external groups to use or how to combine restscore groups. Decisions about whether to delete items and which items to delete should be made on substantive grounds, supported by our statistical tests, rather than by statistical tests alone.

In addition, the requirement of DM can be regarded as a necessary but not sufficient condition of parallel IRFs, as are required in one of the most popular parametric IRT models, the Rasch model.

However, it should be said that Mokken's lower boundary of 0.30 for the coefficient of homogeneity has stood the test of time remarkably well. The higher the homogeneity, the more likely it is that the items in a scale also pass the tests of the probabilistic models.

Therefore, there are three requirements for a set of items to conform to a cumulative scale, based on ordinal IRT: The items should have high enough homogeneity, as discussed in chapter 3; the IRFs should increase monotonely to a sufficient extent (test on monotone homogeneity), as described in chapter 6; and all respondents should agree sufficiently about the order of the items (test on double monotonicity), as described earlier.

CHAPTER 8. CUMULATIVE SCALING WITH POLYTOMOUS ITEMS

In the previous chapters we have constructed a cumulative scale from a set of dichotomous items, each of which divides the latent continuum into two areas. Subjects who give the negative response to the item are represented in the lower area of the continuum, and subjects who give the positive response to the item are represented in the higher area. The two areas along the continuum are separated by a benchmark that forms the border between them. The position of that benchmark indicates the position of the item, denoted as δ_i, the item parameter. Because a dichotomous item has only one benchmark, it has only one item parameter.

In this chapter I show how to apply similar principles to construct a scale consisting of items with three or more ordered response categories, based on ideas developed by Molenaar (1991). An item with three or more ordered categories is called a polytomous item.[1] An example is, "Do you agree or disagree with the following statement: 'People should not have to work if they don't want to.' (1) strongly agree, (2) agree, (3) neither agree nor disagree, (4) disagree, (5) strongly disagree."[2] This item may be regarded as an indicator of a more or less negative or positive attitude toward work. With this item subjects can be represented in five ordered areas along the scale. The five areas are separated by four benchmarks that form the borders between the adjacent response categories. The four benchmarks are now the four parameters of a single item. They can be ordered, for item **i**, as $\delta_{i12} \leq \delta_{i23} \leq \delta_{i34} \leq \delta_{i45}$. Each subject **s** can still be represented by a single parameter, θ_s, because he can be represented in only one of the available areas on the scale. Molenaar suggested referring to a benchmark as an item step. A dichotomous item has one item step, and a polytomous item with k response categories has $k - 1$ item steps.

We will look first at the order of the item steps in the perfect deterministic model. We then examine the concept of model violation and—as in

---

[1] There are also items with three or more response categories that are not ordered, such as "Do you believe in God? (0) No, (1) Don't know, (2) Yes." Here, it is not clear that "Don't know" is intermediate between the other two response categories; it is simply different. Items like these are not called polytomous in the context of IRT and will not be discussed further in this monograph.

[2] This is an example of an item known as a five-point rating scale, or a Likert scale. The term *scale* refers to Likert's contention that the five categories can be interpreted on an interval scale. In this monograph we will use the term *scale* only as a combination of items, in the way psychologists use the word *test*.

chapter 3 for dichotomous items—use a coefficient of homogeneity to compare the amount of model violation observed to the amount expected under statistical independence. This is followed by the use of the concepts of the probabilistic model (MH and DM) to a cumulative scale with polytomous items. Finally, a brief application is given.

8.1 Response Patterns in the Deterministic Cumulative Model for Polytomous Items

Let us return to the first example from chapter 2, where the latent variable itself—people's height—was obvious. We measured height with two dichotomous questions: A: "Are you taller than 1.70 m?" and B: "Are you taller than 1.80 m?" Now we reformulate these questions as a single tri-chotomous (i.e., three-category) question: "How tall are you? Are you (0) shorter than 1.70 m, (1) between 1.70 m and 1.80 m, or (2) taller than 1.80 m?" The answer to this question gives the same information as the answers to the two dichotomous questions taken together; that is, its two benchmarks are the same as the combined single benchmarks of the two dichotomous questions (Figure 8.1a). We will supplement it with a second trichoto-mous height question: "How tall are you? Are you (0) shorter than 1.65 m; (1) between 1.65 m and 1.75 m; or (2) taller than 1.75 m?" This question can again be seen as the combination of two dichotomous ques-tions: A: "Are you taller than 1.65 m?" and B: "Are you taller than 1.75 m?" (Figure 8.1b).

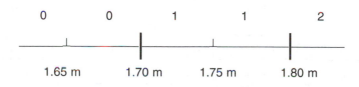

Figure 8.1a Item 1: Shorter than 1.70 m (0), taller than 1.80 m (2), or in between (1).

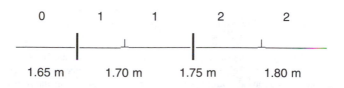

Figure 8.1b Item 2: Shorter than 1.65 m (0), taller than 1.75 m (2), or in between (1).

Because each of the two trichotomous questions has two item steps, the two questions taken together provide four item steps. Following the same logic we just saw, these are equivalent to the benchmarks of four dichotomous items. Taken together, two items with three response categories each can divide a group of subjects into five ordered categories. In our example these are (0) $s < 1.65$ m; (1) 1.65 m $< s < 170$ m; (2) 170 m $< s < 1.75$ m; (3) 1.75 m $< s < 1.80$ m; and (4) $s > 1.80$ m. The latent dimension with the four item steps is visualized in Figure 8.1c.[3]

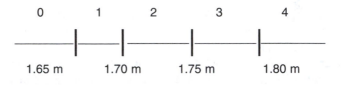

Figure 8.1c Items 1 and 2 taken together: Division into five ordered categories as the sum of the item steps passed from left to right.

As with dichotomous items, it is useful to start the coding of the different response categories with the code 0 and continue on with rank numbers. The codes then specify the number of item steps passed from left to right along the latent continuum. In combining the items (Figure 8.1c) we can combine the number of item steps passed for the two items taken separately (Figures 8.1a and 8.1b) to rank the scale value of the respondent. That is why we show two 0s and two 1s in Figure 8.1a and two 1s and two 2s in Figure 8.1b.

The responses to the two questions are given in Table 8.1. Logically, only five of the nine cells can be filled. These are the five areas on the latent dimension in Figure 8.1c.

Item 1 ↓ Item 2 →	0: <1.65 m	1: 1.65–1.75 m	2: >1.75 m
0: <1.70 m	(0,0): <1.65 m	(0,1): 1.65–1.70 m	
1: 1.70–1.80 m		(1,1): 1.70–1.75 m	(1,2): 1.75–1.80 m
2: >1.80 m			(2,2): >1.80 m

Table 8.1 Cross table with possible responses to the two height items.

---

[3]It would obviously be more straightforward to obtain this information by asking a single five-category question about height than by asking two three-category questions. But recall that it is often not obvious ahead of time whether two or more items measure the same latent variable. The purpose of this treatment of height is didactic, simply to show how trichotomous items in a candidate scale can be combined.

Four cells contain model violations in the example on height; four cells remain empty because their combinations of responses are logically impossible:

(0,2)	shorter than 1.70 m	and taller than 1.75 m
(1,0)	between 1.70 m and 1.80 m	and shorter than 1.65 m
(2,0)	taller than 1.80 m	and shorter than 1.65 m
(2,1)	taller than 1.80 m	and between 1.65 m and 1.75 m

In a 2×2 cross table of two dichotomous items that form a deterministic unidimensional scale, because they measure the same latent variable perfectly, one of the four cells remains empty. In a 3×3 table of two trichotomous items that measure the same latent variable perfectly, four of the nine cells—in this example, cells (0,2), (1,0), (2,0), and (2,1)—remain empty. If we apply this idea to the measurement of social scientific latent variables, we generalize the idea of the Guttman scale, in which only a subset of all possible combinations of responses to polytomous items are allowed.

8.2 Using Social Scientific Items in the Deterministic Cumulative Scale

We will now move to a substantively more interesting example, one that the reader may be able to analyze.[4] The data for this example come from the American section of the World Value Study 2002. They consist of answers to five questions that each have three ordered response categories. The questions were designed to measure a single latent trait of propensity toward political action. They dealt with "A. Signing a petition" (Petition), "B. Joining in boycotts" (Boycott), "C. Attending lawful demonstrations" (Demon), "D. Joining unofficial strikes" (Strike), and "E. Occupying buildings or factories" (Occupy).

For each of these five activities respondents were asked whether they had ever done it ("Have done"), whether they might do it ("Might do"), or whether they would never, under any circumstances, do it ("Would never do"). The original coding has been reversed for our purposes so that the three response categories are ordered from low to high propensity for political action (0 = *Would never do,* 1 = *Might do,* 2 = *Have done*).[5] Subjects who did

---

[4]Assuming that the reader has access to the data and to a statistical package to make cross tables.

[5]In general, researchers are advised to adapt the direction of coding to the direction of the latent trait under scrutiny.

not give a substantive response were deleted from the analyses. $N = 1,110$ subjects remained. Their responses are given in Table 8.2.

The major trick of analyzing polytomous items is to break each item with k response categories up in $k - 1$ dichotomous item steps and to treat these item steps as the new dichotomous items. The order of the item steps can be determined in the same way as the order of the dichotomous items in chapter 7: on the basis of the frequencies of the responses. Subjects who give the response category m to an item (where m is between the lowest category, 0, and the highest category, k) are represented as giving the positive response (1) to item step $m - 1, m$, just as all subjects who responded in a higher category. Subjects who give the response $m - 1$ (or lower) are represented as giving the negative response (0) to item step $m - 1, m$.

Table 8.3 gives the frequencies of the responses to the two item steps for each item, based on the frequencies in Table 8.2. Because these items have three response categories, each item has two item steps, which we shall call the (01) and the (12) item step, respectively. The (01) item step represents the distinction between subjects who would never do a certain political action versus the others, who might do it or who have done it. The (12) item step represents the distinction between subjects who would never do a certain political action or those who might do it, versus the others, who have done it. Finding these frequencies comes down to finding the cumulative frequencies from the lowest category to $m - 1$ as the frequency of the negative response and from category m to k as the frequency of the positive response to that item step. On the basis of these cumulative frequencies we can determine the order of the item steps. As with dichotomous items, the higher the frequency, the more popular or less difficult the item step. If we abbreviate the items with the letters P (for *petition*), B (for *boycotts*), D (for *lawful demonstrations*),

	Would never do (0)	Might do (1)	Have done (2)
A. Signing a petition	34 (3.1%)	168 (15.1%)	908 (81.8%)
B. Joining in boycotts	268 (24.1%)	568 (51.2%)	274 (24.7%)
C. Attending lawful demonstrations	281 (25.3%)	597 (53.8%)	232 (20.9%)
D. Joining unofficial strikes	625 (56.3%)	422 (38.0%)	63 (5.7%)
E. Occupying buildings or factories	786 (70.8%)	277 (25.0%)	47 (4.2%)

Table 8.2 Frequency distribution of five questions about political activity, $N = 1,110$.

	Item step (01) (Never–Might)		Item step (12) (Might–Have)	
	0	1	0	1
A. Signing a **Petition**	34	1,076	202	908
B. Joining in **Boycotts**	268	842	836	274
C. Attending lawful **Demonstrations**	281	829	878	232
D. Joining unofficial **Strikes**	625	485	1,047	63
E. **Occupying** buildings or factories	786	324	1,063	47

Table 8.3 Frequency distribution of the two item steps of the five questions about political activity, $N = 1,110$.

S (for *unofficial strikes*), and O (for *occupying a building*) and we abbreviate the response categories with the letters N (for *would never do*), M (*might do*) and H (*have done*), we can write down the order of the item steps as follows (with the frequency of their positive responses in parentheses):

$$P_{NM} (1,076)—P_{MH} (908)—B_{NM} (842)—D_{NM} (829)—S_{NM} (485)—$$
$$O_{NM} (324)—B_{MH} (274)—D_{MH} (232)—S_{MH} (63)—O_{MH} (47)$$

This order is graphically represented in Figure 8.2.

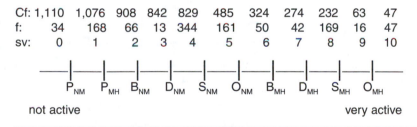

Cf: 1,110 1,076 908 842 829 485 324 274 232 63 47
f: 34   168   66   13 344 161   50   42 169 16 47
sv: 0   1   2   3   4   5   6   7   8   9 10

P_{NM} P_{MH} B_{NM} D_{NM} S_{NM} O_{NM} B_{MH} D_{MH} S_{MH} O_{MH}

not active   very active

Figure 8.2 Benchmarks if the five items form a perfectly deterministic cumulative scale for items P (Petitions), B (Boycotts), D (Demonstrations), S (Strikes), and O (Occupations)—so P_{NM} is the benchmark for item Petitions with categories Never and Might—with cumulative frequencies (Cf) of respondents positioned to the right of a particular item step, frequencies (f) of respondents in a particular area on the scale between two item steps, and scale values (sv).

Based on the information in Table 8.3 and Figure 8.2, it is now possible to reconstruct each of the 10 (5*(5 − 1)/2) cross tables from these five items. Table 8.4 gives the example of the cross table of items B (joining in boycotts) and C (attending lawful demonstrations). The last column and last row give the cumulative frequencies for the two items. Cell (0,0) gives the sum of the frequencies from the left side of the scale to item step B_{NM} (34 + 168 + 66 = 268) (see Figure 8.2). Cell (1,0) gives the frequency of subjects represented in the area between item step B_{NM} and D_{NM} (13). Cell (1,1) gives the sum of the frequencies between D_{NM} and B_{MH} (344 + 161 + 50 = 555). Cell (2,1) gives the frequency of subjects represented between B_{MH} and D_{MH} (42). Cell (2,2) represents the remaining subjects represented to the right of item step D_{MH} (169 + 16 + 47 = 232).

Based on the order of the item steps it is clear which cells in the cross table are filled and which remain empty. These empty cells are the error cells. The comparison of the observed frequency of these cells with the frequency of these cells expected under statistical independence will determine the homogeneity of the item pair as an elementary cumulative scale.

Any item with k response categories (generally between 0 and $k − 1$) will have $(k − 1)$ benchmarks.[6] So two such items taken together will have $2(k − 1)$ benchmarks, which divide the latent continuum into $2(k − 1) + 1$ different areas. But there will be $k * k$ possible response combinations for these two items. If only $2(k − 1) + 1$ of these combinations can be interpreted as valid scale responses, then the remaining $k * k − 2(k − 1) − 1$

Item B: Joining in boycotts	Item C: Attending lawful demonstrations				
	Would never do (0)	Might do (1)	Have done (2)	Total	Cumulative
Would never do (0)	268	0	0	268	1,110
Might do (1)	13 →	555	0	568	842
Have done (2)	0	42 →	232	274	274
Total	281	597	232	1,110	
Cumulative	1,110	829	232		

Table 8.4 Cross table of two political activity items in a perfect cumulative scale.

[6]For instance, a Likert scale item with five response categories (0, 1, 2, 3, and 4) has four item steps: (01), (12), (23), and (34).

cannot. These combinations violate the cumulative model. As the number of response categories m increases, so do the number of possible model violations. If k is 2, only 1 of the 4 response combinations is a model violation; if k is 3, then 4 of the 9 combinations are model violations. For $k = 4$, it is 9 out of 16, and for $k = 5$, it is 16 out of 25. Which of the combinations are valid and which are model violations depends on the order of the benchmarks, or item steps.

8.3 Evaluating Homogeneity

Table 8.5 gives the empirical cross table of these two political action questions from the data of the American section of the World Values Study. The order of the item steps was given in Figure 8.2, so the following four response combinations must be model violations: (0,1), Never, Might; (0,2), Never, Have; (1,2), Might, Have; and (2,0), Have, Never. In the table the frequencies in these four cells are written in italics.

In our social scientific example the response combinations that contain model violations are not logically impossible and they (empirically) do occur. However, they do falsify the cumulative model that we use to measure a single latent variable. In order to evaluate the seriousness of the model violations—or the lack of homogeneity—we compare them, as in chapter 3 for dichotomous items, to the number of model violations that we would have expected if the items are statistically independent. In the case of insufficient homogeneity the items do not form a cumulative scale.

Table 8.6 gives the frequencies expected if the two items are statistically independent. These frequencies are found by multiplying the row and column marginal frequencies for each cell and dividing the result by the total number of cases. For example, the expected frequency of cell (0,0), Never,

Item B: Joining in boycotts	Item C: Attending lawful demonstrations			
	Would never do (0)	Might do (1)	Have done (2)	Total
Would never do (0)	149	*101*	*18*	268
Might do (1)	99	395	*74*	568
Have done (2)	*33*	101	140	274
Total	281	597	232	1,110

Table 8.5 Cross table of joining in boycotts and attending lawful demonstrations.

Item B: Joining in boycotts	Item C: Attending lawful demonstrations			
	Would never do (0)	Might do (1)	Have done (2)	Total
Would never do (0)	67.8	*144.1*	*56.0*	268
Might do (1)	143.8	305.5	*118.7*	568
Have done (2)	*69.4*	147.4	57.3	274
Total	281	597	232	1,110

Table 8.6 Cross table of cell frequencies expected if items Boycotts and Demonstrations are statistically independent.

Never, is (281 * 268)/1,110 = 67.8. As in Table 8.5, the frequencies of the error cells are written in italics.

In the four cells that constitute model violations, the frequencies expected if answers to the two questions are independent of each other are: cell (0,1), 144.1; cell (0,2), 56.0; cell (1,2), 118.7; and cell (2,0), 69.4.

It is not useful to inspect the number of errors in each of the four error cells separately. They need to be combined so that an overall verdict can be reached for the pair of items. This is because the researcher must decide whether an item as a whole—as opposed to its individual item steps—is sufficiently homogeneous with the other items in the scale to be retained. The simplest way to make this decision is to simply add up the number of errors observed in the four cells and compare this sum with the sum of errors expected under statistical independence. As in chapter 3, we first discuss the homogeneity of a pair of items and subsequently the homogeneity of individual items, which is based on the pairs of items in which they appear.

From the empirical cross table (Table 8.5) we get the number of errors observed as Err(obs) = 101 + 18 + 74 + 33 = 226. And the number of errors expected under statistical independence, Err(exp), can be found from the statistically independent cross table (Table 8.6): Err(exp) = 144.1 + 56.0 + 118.7 + 69.4 = 388.2. Just as in the case of dichotomous items (see chapter 3), the coefficient of homogeneity is defined as follows:

$$\mathbf{H}(ij) = 1 - \frac{\text{Err(obs)}}{\text{Err(exp)}}$$

In this case, then, **H**(*ij*) is $1 - 226/388.2 = 0.42$. Before we continue with determining the homogeneity of a scale with more than two items, and the homogeneity of individual items, let us take a closer look at the four cells that contain model violations for this pair of items. Are some model violations more serious than others? Cell (0,2), for instance, seems to be worse than either cell (0,1) or cell (1,2), because this cell is further away from the perfect pathway shown in Table 8.4. Should we take such differences into account? Molenaar (1991) proposed to weight model violations by considering the order of the item steps.

A weighted coefficient of homogeneity. Let us take two items **i** and **j** with three response categories each (0, 1, and 2), and let us assume that the order of the item steps is **i**(01), **j**(01), **i**(12), **j**(12). The five admissible response patterns now are (0,0), (1,0), (1,1), (2,1), and (2,2). And the four inadmissible error patterns are (0,1), (0,2), (1,2), and (2,0) (Table 8.7).

When we order the item steps, we can create Table 8.8. The first column gives the response to both items, the first response to item **i**, the second to

Item i ↓ Item j →	0	1	2
0	(0,0)	*error*	*error*
1	(1,0)	(1,1)	*error*
2	*error*	(2,1)	(2,2)

Table 8.7 Cross table showing the item steps passed from (top) left to (bottom) right.

Response **i,j**	**i**(01)	**j**(01)	**i**(12)	**j**(12)
0,0	0	0	0	0
1,0	1	0	0	0
1,1	1	1	0	0
2,1	1	1	1	0
2,2	1	1	1	1

Table 8.8 Data matrix in which item steps take on the role of new dichotomous variables.

item **j**. The second column indicates whether a person can be represented to the left (0) or right (1) of item step **i**(01), based only on his response to item **i**. Similarly, the third, fourth, and fifth columns indicate whether the person can be represented to the left (0) or right (1) of item steps **j**(01), **i**(12), and **j**(12), respectively.

A person who gives the 0 response to item **i** not only is represented to the left of item step **i**(01)—and therefore gets the code 0 on item step **i**(01)—but also is necessarily represented to the left of item step **i**(12), so he also gets the code 0 on item step **i**(12). On the other hand, a person who gives the 2 response to item **i** is represented to the right of item step **i**(12) and gets the code 1 for that, but he necessarily is also represented to the right of item step **i**(01), for which he also then gets the code 1. The same rule applies to all items.

The item steps can now be regarded as new dichotomous items that differ in their difficulty: The farther to the right in Table 8.8, the more difficult. The codes 1 and 0 can be regarded as giving the positive or negative response to a particular item step. And according to the cumulative scaling model, a positive response to a more difficult item (step) implies a positive response to all easier items (steps). So the appropriate combinations of responses can be represented as a lower triangle of 1s and an upper triangle of 0s, just as in the case of the Guttman scale for dichotomous items.

Let us now see what happens with the inadmissible response combinations.

The response **ij**(0,1) is coded in Table 8.9 as 0–1–0–0. So the more difficult item step **j**(01) gets the positive response, and the easier item step **i**(01) gets the negative response. This combination of codes, **i**(01)/**j**(01), is therefore a model violation, according to the transitivity requirements discussed in chapter 3. Therefore, the response **ij**(0,1) leads to an error. Response combination **ij**(0,2) is worse, because it leads to three inadmissible combinations of codes, **i**(01)/**j**(01), **i**(01)/**j**(12), and **i**(12)/**j**(12), and so to three errors. Response combinations **ij**(1,2), and **ij**(2,0) again lead to one error each, **i**(12)/**j**(12) and **j**(01)/**i**(12), respectively.

The number of errors that are made in an inadmissible response combination is called the *weight* of that response combination. In order to determine homogeneity, we will multiply both the number of errors observed and errors expected by that weight.

We take the example of the item pair Boycotts and Demonstrations, where we know the order of the item steps from Figure 8.2, and the frequency of errors in each of the four error cells from Table 8.5. The results are found in Table 8.10.

In this example the weighted coefficient of homogeneity $(1 - 262/500.2 = 0.48)$ is even better than the unweighted coefficient $(1 - 226/388.2 = 0.42)$. Note that the weight of an error cell depends on the order of the item steps.

Response **i,j**	**i(01)**	**j(01)**	**i(12)**	**j(12)**	Number of errors
0,1	0	1	0	0	1
0,2	0	1	0	1	3
1,2	1	1	0	1	1
2,0	1	0	1	0	1

Table 8.9 New data matrix containing model violations.

Response (B,C)	E(obs)	E(exp)	B_{NM}	D_{NM}	B_{MH}	D_{MH}	W = # errors	W * E(obs)	W * E(exp)
0 0			0	0	0	0	0	0	0
0 1*	101	144.1	0	1	0	0	1	101	144.1
0 2*	18	56.0	0	1	0	1	3	54	168
1 0			1	0	0	0	0		
1 1			1	1	0	0	0		
1 2*	74	118.7	1	1	0	1	1	74	118.7
2 0*	33	69.4	1	0	1	0	1	33	69.4
2 1			1	1	1	0	0		
2 2			1	1	1	1	0		
Total	226	388.2						262	500.2

Table 8.10 Calculating the weighted **H** coefficient for the item pair Boycott–Demonstrations.

Homogeneity of the scale and of individual items. Once the concept of homogeneity of an item pair is understood, as is the role that item steps play in the determination of model violation and the weight of a model violation, the further generalization to determining the homogeneity of the scale and of individual items becomes simpler, because it follows the same logic as was explained in chapter 3 for dichotomous items. For instance, for determining the homogeneity of the whole scale we need to sum the weighted number of errors observed and expected. They are given in Table 8.11. The sum of Err(Obs) = 1,544, the sum of Err(Exp) = 2,723.9, so $\mathbf{H} = 1 - 1,544/2,723.9 = 0.43$. For item Petition, the relevant numbers are sum of Err(Obs) = 390, sum of Err(Exp) = 658.3, so $\mathbf{H} = 1 - 390/658.3 = 0.41$.

Table 8.12 gives the pairwise $\mathbf{H}(ij)$ coefficients in its lower triangle. In its upper triangle we find the $Z(ij)$ values, which have the same interpretation as in chapter 3 and Appendix 1. As long as $Z(ij)$ is higher than a critical lower boundary, generally based on an alpha level of 0.05, we regard the $\mathbf{H}(ij)$ coefficient as statistically significant. Note that all $\mathbf{H}(ij)$ values are positive, and on the whole rather high, with the exception of item pair (Petition, Occupy). Because this $\mathbf{H}(ij)$ value is low (0.05), the $Z(ij)$ value is also low (0.44).

	Petition	Boycott	Demonstration	Strike	Occupy
Petition		237.3	225.6	116.5	78.9
Boycott	110		500.2	334.0	319.0
Demonstration	140	262		319.2	295.4
Strike	65	174	147		297.8
Occupy	75	239	178	154	

Table 8.11 Item (pair Boycott, Demonstrations). Lower triangle, number of weighted observed errors; upper triangle, number of weighted expected errors.

	Petition	Boycott	Demonstration	Strike	Occupy
Petition		11.43	7.91	5.36	0.44
Boycott	0.54		15.08	11.40	6.20
Demonstration	0.38	0.48		12.63	9.37
Strike	0.44	0.48	0.54		12.91
Occupy	0.05	0.25	0.40	0.48	

Table 8.12 Coefficient of homogeneity $\mathbf{H}(ij)$ in lower triangle, and $Z(ij)$ in upper triangle for each item pair.

8.4 The Search Procedure for Polytomous Items

As discussed in Chapter 4 with dichotomous items, the search procedure for finding a cumulative scale with polytomous items is a bottom-up procedure. This begins (at the bottom) with the smallest possible scale, i.e., a scale of two (polytomous) items. Among all item pairs the pair with the highest H(ij) is sought (see Table 8.12: it is pair (Demonstrations, Strike) with a H(ij) of 0.539. H(ij) of pair (Petition, Boycott) is just marginally lower, 0.536. This value is positive, it is higher than the default lower boundary of 0.30, and it is statistically significant (its Z(ij) value is higher than 2). As more items are added to the scale, the homogeneity of the scale and of all items in the scale drops, whereas the Z-values increase (see Table 8.13). The last item, Occupy, still has a high enough H(i) coefficient, and the low pairwise H(ij)-coefficients with items Petitions and Boycotts are offset sufficiently by the higher values for pairs with items Demonstrations and Strikes. There are no negative H(ij)-values, so no negative correlations, and no item is rejected from the scale. In addition, all H(i)values are high enough so than no item gets excluded.

Item	Mean	Step 1		Step 2		Step 3		Step 4	
		H(i)	Z(i)	H(i)	Z(i)	H(i)	Z(i)	H(i)	Z(i)
Demons	0.96	0.54	12.63	0.50	19.67	0.47	21.10	0.46	23.03
Strike	0.49	0.54	12.63	0.51	16.98	0.50	17.60	0.49	21.55
Boycott	1.01	...	...	0.48	18.84	0.49	22.00	0.44	22.30
Petition	1.79	...	...	...	...	0.46	14.48	0.41	13.23
Occupy	0.33	...	...	...	...	...	...	0.35	15.05
SCALE		0.54	12.63	0.49	22.68	0.48	26.86	0.43	30.55
Rejected items	None		None		None		None		

Table 8.13 Short history of hierarchical clustering (search) procedure.

The result of this search procedure is given in Table 8.14 as the final scale. The difference with Table 8.13 is the order in which the items are represented, namely according to their mean value, from low to high. In analogy to a scale with dichotomous items we can interpret this order in terms of their cumulativity: a high value on the first ('most difficult') item implies a high value on all 'easier' items represented lower down.

For polytomous items this is only an approximate description, because here we are interested in the order of the item steps, rather than of the items as a whole.

Item	Mean	Item H	Z
Occupying buildings or factories	0.33	0.35	15.05
Joining unofficial strikes	0.49	0.49	21.55
Attending lawful demonstrations	0.96	0.46	23.03
Joining in boycotts	1.01	0.44	22.30
Signing a petition	1.79	0.41	13.23

Table 8.14 Final scale (N=1110, H=0.43, Z=30.55, critical Z = 2.73).

8.5 Applying the Probabilistic Model to Polytomous Items

The check for MH showed that there were no violations larger than 0.03, when we used restscore groups of at least 50 subjects. We show one result in detail, in order to show which pairs of restscore groups were compared (Table 8.15). First of all, restscore groups with scores 0 and 1 were combined, just as restscore groups with the scores 7 and 8, to form groups of at least 50 subjects. In an item with three response categories, two item steps can be distinguished, the (01) and the (12) step. The Item Step Response Functions are given by the proportion of positive response to these item steps for each of the restscore groups. For the first restscore group (group 1, scores are 0 or 1, $N = 61$) the proportion of subjects in this group that have 'passed' item step (01) is $(2 + 1)/61 = 0.05$. The proportion of subjects that 'passed' item step (12) is just $1/61 = 0.02$. For item step (01) all proportions increase from the lowest to the highest restscore group. For item step (12) there is a violation of 0.02 (so below the default value of 0.03) between restscore groups 1 and 2. Note that for item step (01) comparisons can be made among all pairs of 7 restscore groups, or 21 appropriate comparisons. For item step (12) the proportion of positive responses to restscore group 2 is exactly 0.00, so this group is not involved in other comparisons, with one exception. This leaves the comparison between all pairs of 6 restscore groups, or 15 groups. The exception is the comparison between groups 1 and 2, which brings the total number of appropriate comparisons for this item step function to 16, and the total number of appropriate comparisons to $21 + 16 = 37$.

```
Strike   Joining unofficial strikes
Restscore                Frequencies per                    Proportions
                                                            of positive
group   Low High      N        item value      Mean     responses per
                                                            item step
                             0     1    2              ≥1      ≥2
   1     0  -  1      61     58     2    1    0.07     0.05    0.02
   2           2     126    108    18    0    0.14     0.14    0.00
   3           3     182    129    48    5    0.32     0.29    0.03
   4           4     323    212   106    5    0.36     0.34    0.02
   5           5     206     70   126   10    0.71     0.66    0.05
   6           6     131     42    70   19    0.82     0.68    0.15
   7     7  -  8      81      6    52   23    1.21     0.93    0.28
```

Table 8.15 Results for the check on monotone homogeneity for item Strike.

The check of DM, using restscore groups of at least 50 subjects, leads to a number of violations, some of which are significant. These results are summarized in Table 8.16.

```
Summary per item for check of nonintersection via restscore groups
Minimum violation = 0.03   Sig. level = 0.05   Minimum group
size = 50

           Item H  #ac #vi #vi/#ac maxvi  sum  sum/#ac zmax #zsig crit
Petition    0.41   72   2     0.03 0.09 0.17 0.0024  3.08    2    46
Boycott     0.44   64   5     0.08 0.09 0.33 0.0051  2.70    1    48
Demons      0.46   64   5     0.08 0.09 0.35 0.0055  3.08    1    49*
Strike      0.49   72   1     0.01 0.07 0.07 0.0010  1.21    0     9
Occupy      0.35   72   3     0.04 0.07 0.17 0.0024  1.22    0    23
```

Table 8.16 Summary of results of check of double monotonicity (nonintersection of item response functions) using restscore groups of at least 50 subjects, with a minimum amount of violation of 0.03.

The largest violation (maxvi) is between item step Demonstration (01) and Petition (12) (Table 8.17). It occurs for restscore group 4 (with restscore 3): the violation is 0.09 (0.96 − 0.86) and has a significant z value of 3.08. However, because the crit values remain low enough, this is not enough reason to discard any of the items.

86

```
I = (Demons    >1) with list below
-----------------------------------
J = (Petition >2)
```

Restscore Low/High Group		N	Frequencies for item step pair IJ 00	01	10	11	vi	z	Proportions of positive responses per item step Demons >1	Petition >2
1	0–0	194	51	70	25	48			0.38	0.61
2	1–1	314	21	63	37	193			0.73	0.82
3	2–2	268	9	53	25	181			0.77	0.87
4	3–3	200	2	7	25	166	0.09	3.08	0.96	0.86
5	4–6	134	2	3	5	124			0.96	0.95
Total		1,110	85	196	117	712	0.09		0.75	0.82

Table 8.17 Details of largest model violation in this example.

Tests for DM using the P(+,+) and P(−,−) matrix show no further signs of serious model violations. In fact, the P matrices show no violations at all. The reliability according to Mokken's method is 0.72.

8.6 The Scale of Political Action

Table 8.18 gives the scale values of the 1,110 subjects without missing values to the scale of political action. A majority of subjects are found with scale values between 4 and 8: They do sign petitions, and they might join boycotts and lawful demonstrations, but they are not too keen on joining unofficial strikes and occupying buildings and factories. The distribution of scale scores is close to normal (skewness = −0.16, kurtosis = −0.22). Very few people give the same response to all five items: 7 will do nothing, 20 have done everything.

Half of the subjects made no Guttman errors at all, and only one (subject 34) made 11 errors: He has occupied a building and might sign a petition but would never join a boycott, attend a lawful demonstration, or join in an unofficial strike (Table 8.19).

It is now possible to determine who is more politically active than others. We might also correlate the scale value with the number of Guttman errors. There is no reason to expect that these two variables should be highly correlated, and they are only marginally so: $r = 0.085$ ($p = .005$ with $N = 1,110$); higher scale values give a slightly higher probability of more Guttman errors.

	Scale score		Guttman errors	
	Frequency	Percentage	Frequency	Percentage
0	–	–	552	50
1	–	–	147	13
2	–	–	162	15
3	–	–	105	9
4	–	–	71	6
5	7	1	37	3
6	25	2	9	1
7	64	6	5	0
8	84	8	5	0
9	173	16	11	1
10	181	16	5	0
11	260	23	1	0
12	148	13	–	–
13	110	10	–	–
14	38	3	–	–
15	20	2	–	–
Mean	10.4	100%	1.4	100%
Standard deviation	2.0		1.9	

Table 8.18 Scale scores and number of Guttman errors for the scale of unparliamentary political action.

P_{01}	P_{12}	B_{01}	D_{01}	S_{01}	O_{01}	B_{12}	D_{12}	S_{12}	O_{12}
1	0	0	0	0	1	0	0	0	1

Table 8.19 Response pattern of subject 34 with 11 model violations, dichotomously coded according to the 10 ordered item steps.

CHAPTER 9. REMAINING ISSUES

In this chapter we take on two remaining issues. The first is the comparison of our ordinal IRT model with other measurement models, and the second is what to do with nondiscriminating response patterns. As other measurement models we will discuss reliability analysis and factor analysis on one hand and parametric IRT, especially the one parameter logistic model, also known as the Rasch model (Andrich, 1988; Ostini & Nering, 2006; Rasch, 1960/1980), on the other. These other models may lead to different results, so we need to understand why that might happen. Nondiscriminating response patterns play a fundamentally different role in these other models, and their treatment in our ordinal IRT model warrants discussion. The chapter follows with a discussion of two practical matters: How do we use the scale values of subjects, and can we use items with different numbers of response categories? We end with some final remarks.

9.1 Reliability Analysis

Homogeneity versus reliability. The concept of homogeneity in ordinal cumulative scale analysis is different from the concept of reliability in reliability analysis. By *homogeneity* we mean that different items measure the same latent trait. By *reliability* we mean that when the same question is asked again, the researcher will obtain the same response. Because it is not good practice to ask the same question twice—at least not in the same survey—it is difficult to establish reliability of measurement. Researchers have therefore taken to asking similar (or parallel) questions and treating them as if they were the same. They then establish their reliability, which is better understood as their homogeneity.

Mokken's estimation of reliability. Mokken (1971) came up with an ingenious way to estimate the reliability of a cumulative scale. He used the P(+,+) matrix—which we used in chapter 6 to check the model assumption of DM—to estimate the proportion of subjects who would have given the same response to a particular item twice. This proportion is obviously not available, but it might be found on the diagonal of the P(+,+) matrix. If the P(+,+) matrix conforms to the requirement of double monotonicity, then cell proportions in each row or column are monotonely increasing, and the values for the proportions on the diagonal can be estimated by extrapolation (for the two outer items) and interpolation (for the remaining items). These proportions are then used in the formula for the reliability (as the ratio of true variance over observed variance). Appendix 3 explains Mokken's approach to reliability and gives a numerical example for the five dichotomous items of our example of American religious beliefs from chapter 5.

Correlations and their problems. Reliability is most easily calculated in terms of the average correlation coefficient, r_{av}, among all items, assuming that they have the same standard deviation:

$$\text{Reliability } \rho = \frac{k * r_{av}}{1 + (k - 1) * r_{av}} \text{ (where } k \text{ is the number of items)}$$

The higher the average correlation among all items, the higher their reliability. Reliability can also be increased by adding items to a scale, as long as the average correlation does not decrease too much. Adding items will generally not increase the homogeneity of a scale. The use of the correlation matrix implies that the researcher assumes that the answers to his items are measured along an interval scale. The justification for this is discussed later.

It has been known for a long time (Carroll, 1945; Ferguson, 1941) that problems with the use of the correlation coefficient can occur when the items are not parallel, that is, do not have the same means and standard deviation. This problem will be illustrated with a hypothetical dataset, shown in Table 9.1 (see van Schuur, 2003, for a similar example). A hundred subjects responded to six dichotomous items. Seven perfectly cumulative response patterns occur with the frequencies given in the last column. Let us imagine that D, E, and F are three variables that tap voting behavior in three elections in which almost everybody votes, whereas A, B, and C measure voting behavior in three secondary elections. The last three items are very popular—most subjects report engaging in the activity ($p_D = .89$, $p_E = .95$, and $p_F = .99$)—and the first three items are much less popular ($p_A = .45$, $p_B = .51$, and $p_C = .55$). The correlations and the coefficients of homogeneity are given in Table 9.2. The homogeneity for all item pairs is perfect, but the correlations differ in size, from the highest around the diagonal to the lowest in the bottom-left corner. These correlations are the highest possible, given the marginal frequency distributions of the items.

In this dataset, the reliability (Cronbach's α) of the scale of six items is 0.82, but it could be increased to 0.85 by removing item 6, or, in fact, to 0.96 by removing the last three items. The last three items therefore deteriorate the reliability of the first three items, whereas all six of them form a perfect cumulative scale.

Response type	A	B	C	D	E	F	Frequency of occurrence of response pattern
1	0	0	0	0	0	0	1
2	0	0	0	0	0	1	4
3	0	0	0	0	1	1	6
4	0	0	0	1	1	1	34
5	0	0	1	1	1	1	4
6	0	1	1	1	1	1	6
7	1	1	1	1	1	1	45
	45	51	55	89	95	99	100

Table 9.1 Hypothetical dataset conforming to a perfect cumulative scale.

	Correlations						Homogeneity coefficients				
	A	B	C	D	E		A	B	C	D	E
B	.89					B	1.0				
C	.82	.92				C	1.0	1.0			
D	.32	.36	.39			D	1.0	1.0	1.0		
E	.21	.23	.23	.65		E	1.0	1.0	1.0	1.0	
F	.09	.10	.10	.29	.44	F	1.0	1.0	1.0	1.0	1.0

Table 9.2 Correlations and homogeneity coefficients for the data shown in Table 9.1.

9.2 Factor Analysis

Factor analysis is the second measurement model with which our ordinal IRT model should be compared.[1] Loosely formulated, factor analysis can

---

[1] We will not distinguish between factor analysis and principal component analysis here, and we use *factor analysis* as the more generic term.

be regarded as a generalization of reliability analysis. Among a set of items it tries to find clusters of items that each could form a reliable scale, with high intracluster (or intrafactor) correlations. The problems with using correlations, the value of which depends on the distribution of the variables, are as noticeable in factor analysis as they are in reliability analysis. A factor analysis of the dataset in Table 9.1 leads to two rather than one factor with eigenvalues larger than 1. The varimax rotated solution leads to the results given in Table 9.3, in which the more difficult first three and the easier last three items load on separate factors.

The results of either a reliability analysis or a factor analysis of this dataset would have cast serious doubts on the unidimensionality of the six variables. Proponents of factor analysis might nevertheless be able to find the unidimensional cumulative pattern in the data, by pointing out that all six items load highly on the first unrotated factor (not shown), that one might interpret the two factors as difficulty factors, that a lower boundary of an eigenvalue of 1.00 for the substantive interpretation of a factor may be too low, or that one should use polychoric rather than product–moment correlations. But this requires understanding that the application of factor analysis to data that suit a cumulative model is not straightforward.

In factor analysis and reliability analysis the assumption that the items can be regarded as parallel, that is, as having the same frequency distribution (the same mean and standard deviation) is fundamentally violated in a cumulative scale: Items *do* differ in their frequency distribution. This difference constitutes the rationale for a cumulative scale, and it is the reason why a factor analysis of dichotomous data is difficult to interpret. The order of difficulty of the items often has an important theoretical

	Factor 1	*Factor 2*
V1	0.93	0.10
V2	0.97	0.13
V3	0.94	0.16
V4	0.31	0.76
V5	0.13	0.88
V6	−0.03	0.72

Table 9.3 Varimax rotated factor loadings of dataset in Table 9.1.

interpretation that is not taken into consideration in reliability and factor analyses. For instance, if it shows in a scale that measures affluence, as in chapter 2, that it is easier to own a CD player than a dishwasher, then the researcher may infer that consumers buy a CD player before they buy a dishwasher. Such an inference cannot be made on the basis of a reliability or factor analysis. If items form a cumulative scale, or are expected to do so, it makes sense to analyze them with a model that takes the relevant model assumption into account.

A second advantage of the ordinal IRT model over factor analysis is that factor analysis always has a solution, that is, one always finds at least one factor, because—except in the unlikely situation that all items are perfectly independent—there will always be at least one factor with a largest eigen-value, larger than 1, which is not necessarily substantively interpretable. In ordinal IRT analysis, however, it is perfectly possible for all $H(ij)$ values to fall below the user-specified lower boundary, so that no scale is found.

9.3 A Parametric IRT Model: The Rasch Model

The ordinal IRT model should be compared not only with reliability analy-sis and factor analysis but also with parametric IRT models that are more popular in some disciplines such as education. The ordinal IRT models discussed in this volume are called nonparametric, because their parameters are only the order of the items and the order of the subjects. In parametric IRT models, in contrast, subject and item parameters are measurement val-ues on an interval scale. More important, however, is that one particular parametric model—known as the simple logistic model or the one-parameter logistic model—has specific desirable measurement properties. In this model the measurement of the subjects does not depend on the specific items used, and the model allows the comparison of scales in which only some but not all of the items are identical. It is sometimes called the Rasch model, after its founder, Danish statistician Georg Rasch (1960/1980).

The property of the Rasch model that is most advantageous is called specific objectivity or item(/subject) invariance. This means that the esti-mation of the item parameters does not depend on the specific subjects in the analysis, and the estimation of the subject parameters does not depend on the specific items. Specific objectivity is a consequence of specifying the IRFs as parallel logistic functions. The property of specific objectivity comes with several advantages. For example, the investigator can conduct tailor-made testing, because subjects do not need to answer all the test items but only the items with approximately the same value on the scale as the subjects' own value. This makes it possible to combine different tests, as long as there are a few shared items to allow calibration. The property of specific objectivity and the potential for tailor-made testing make the Rasch model an important model in the field of psychological and educational measurement, where the measurements must be precise and reliable enough to make decisions about individual subjects. Because of the need for precision and reliability, tests based on the Rasch model are generally longer than the measurement instruments found in most survey research.

If the Rasch model fits, then it is a very desirable measurement model. But the model fits only if its assumptions are met, and the assumption of parallel logistic IRFs is very (often too) strict. The Rasch model may be regarded as a special case of the DM model, but with a few reservations. First, the Rasch model does not use subjects who do not discriminate, that is, who give the same response to all items. This point will be elaborated later. Second, even if the data have no structure (i.e., they are random data), the Rasch model fits those data (Wood, 1978). Random data do not conform to the ordinal IRT model, however, because of insufficient homogeneity. On the other hand, a perfect Guttman scale cannot be a good Rasch scale, because when nondiscriminating subjects and items are discarded, nothing is left.

9.4 Applying the Other Measurement Models to the American Belief Data

Both reliability analysis and factor analysis need the correlation matrix, which is given in Table 9.4a. For comparison, the matrix with homogeneity values is given in Table 9.4b. The homogeneity values are higher than the correlations, and in the correlation matrix, in which the row and column items are ordered according to their popularity, the correlation between items generally decreases for items that are more different in their distribution.

	Correlations					Homogeneity coefficients			
	Hell	Life	Heaven	Soul		Hell	Life	Heaven	Soul
Life	0.32				Life	0.36			
Heaven	0.64	0.39			Heaven	0.96	0.52		
Soul	0.34	0.35	0.43		Soul	0.86	0.80	0.72	
God	0.34	0.27	0.49	0.39	God	0.87	0.63	0.86	0.40
a.					b.				

Table 9.4 Correlations and homogeneity coefficients, all subjects, $N = 1,200$.

A reliability analysis carried out on these data gives a Cronbach's alpha of 0.743. If the worst item (Life) were deleted, Cronbach's alpha would still be 0.738. A factor analysis on the same data gives only one factor, and all five factor loadings are high (Table 9.5):

Hell	0.75
Life	0.62
Heaven	0.85
Soul	0.69
God	0.69

Table 9.5 Factor loadings on first factor.

However, the Rasch model used on our American religious belief items does not fit.[2]

9.5 Nondiscriminating Response Patterns

Why does the Rasch model not fit, although the items form a nice cumulative scale, a reliable test, and a well-defined factor? The answer lies in whether the information is used of the 28 people who did not give a positive response to any item and the 716 people who gave the positive response to all items (see Table 5.8 in chapter 5). In the Rasch model people need to discriminate between the items in order to determine the distances between the items, and items need to discriminate (i.e., items for which everybody either gives the positive or negative answer are useless) in order to determine the distance between the subjects. So the Rasch model uses only the 456 subjects who did discriminate, and it found a badly fitting scale.

For a reliability analysis nothing is better than subjects giving the same (reliable) response over and over again. Respondents who do not discriminate are the backbone of a reliability analysis. High correlations can be obtained only if subjects who give a particular score to one item will give the same score to other items. Surely there is no good reason to delete such subjects. However, if we repeated the reliability analysis for only the 456 discriminating respondents, we would find a reliability of 0.19, and only two items—Hell and Heaven—would form a scale with a reliability of 0.60.

---

[2]We get the same results from the RUMM2030, OPLM, or WINMIRA programs.

	Correlations					Homogeneity coefficients			
	Hell	Life	Heaven	Soul		Hell	Life	Heaven	Soul
Life	−.50				Life	−.64			
Heaven	.43	−.01			Heaven	.90	−.01		
Soul	.10	.11	.18		Soul	.48	.40	.40	
God	.10	−.04	.30	−.07	God	.51	−.15	.69	−.08
a.					b.				

Table 9.6 Correlations and homogeneity coefficients, only discriminating subjects, $N = 456$.

A factor analysis would give three factors with eigenvalues larger than 1. And the ordinal IRT model would also break down. Table 9.6 shows the correlations and the homogeneity coefficients for this analysis.

A cumulative scale can be found for the three items Hell, Heaven, and God, and the other two items (Life and Soul) form a second scale. Note that item Soul does not form part of the first scale, because the homogeneity coefficient of one of the six item pairs (Soul, God) is negative (−.08).

As this example has shown, it can make a world of difference whether or not nondiscriminating subjects are included in an analysis. The treatment of nondiscriminating subjects is a matter of serious debate: Do they justify the reliability model, or do they artificially increase the homogeneity of the scale, because nondiscriminating respondents cannot falsify the assumed cumulativity in the data? For scales with a small number of items, deleting the nondiscriminating subjects seems like a bad idea, because in relative terms they often make up a substantial proportion of subjects. But for scales with many items, nondiscriminating subjects make up a smaller proportion of all respondents, and the cumulative model should fit anyway. It is not possible to give an unequivocal recommendation about what to do, except to understand that the researcher needs to make a conscious decision about whether to include or exclude nondiscriminating respondents.

9.6 Some Practical Matters

Scale scores: Ordinal or metric? In this monograph I have emphasized that our procedure is ordinal and not metric. The result is ordered items or item steps and (partially) ordered subjects (subjects with the same score are tied). But many statistical procedures, such as regression analysis, require subjects to be measured on a metric scale. So can we use the scale scores—which are the end product of our scale analysis—for further statistical analyses?

I believe that we can, basing our work on the literature that begins with Rensis Likert's seminal 1932 article. Likert compared z scores as measurements for response categories with -2, -1, 0, $+1$, $+2$ scores as truncated integers (to which one may add values such as 2 or 3 without changing the metric interpretation of the scores) of five-point rating scales. This comes down to an ordinal transformation of these original z scores. He concluded that further statistical results based on truncated data were no worse than the original results. This finding made him the champion of quantitative survey research of the 20th century, because five-point rating scales could now be considered as interval data. In applications of ordinal IRT we generalize Likert's finding. Both reliability analysis and ordinal IRT use the unweighted sum score of the answers to the items as the scale score for subjects. If ordinal transformations do not seriously change the substantive interpretations of further statistical analyses, then we can also apply Likert's conclusion to our subject scale values, as interpretable as interval values and usable in the most common linear statistical models, such as factor analysis and regression analysis.

Application to items with different response categories. In this monograph, as in most other introductions, all the items that form a scale have the same number of response categories. But is this really necessary? The verdict is not yet in on this question. Recall that increasing benchmarks or item steps are the fundamental building blocks of a cumulative scale. This suggests that it should methodologically be possible to use items with different response categories in a single scale; technically it already is. Note that the model contains no assumptions about the order of distances between the response categories for different items.

9.7 Some Final Remarks

Ordinal IRT started with Mokken's dissertation, published in 1971, and is therefore better known as Mokken scale analysis. Mokken published several additional papers (e.g., Mokken, 1997; Mokken & Lewis, 1982), as did some of his students (e.g., Niemöller & van Schuur, 1983; van Schuur, 2003). However, most new developments came from his friend and colleague Ivo Molenaar, Molenaar's student Klaas Sijtsma, and students of Sijtsma, such as Bas Hemker and Andries van der Ark. These methods are still under development. Sijtsma and Molenaar's (2002) monograph is at present the standard introduction to the technique.

Software for Mokken scale analysis was first (in the 1960s) developed under the name Scale Analysis Method Mokken (SCAMMO) by Han Hol and then (in the 1970s) incorporated in the Statistical Appendix (STAP) to SPSS as MOKKEN SCALE by Wim van Hoboken and Pierre Debets. A new Windows program, MSP, was developed by Peter Boer under the supervision of Rob Mokken, Ivo Molenaar, Klaas Sijtsma, and Wijbrandt van Schuur. Others have made standalone programs in other programming languages, or adaptations for SPSSX, STATA, or R: Kingma and Taerum (1989), Rivas and Martinez (1992), Rivas, Martinez, and Hidalgo (1996), Van der Ark (2007), and Weesie (1999).

Applications initially came from a small circle of researchers around Mokken, Molenaar, and Sijtsma, with additional help from summer courses on scale analysis and dimensional analysis at the Inter-University Consortium for Political and Social Research Summer School in Ann Arbor, the Essex Summer School in Social Science Data Analysis and Collection, and the Brussels Quantitative Analysis in the Social Sciences program. Today, a host of applications can be found, especially in the field of medical sociology. Other applications exist in the field of economic psychology, political science, and education. Ordinal IRT can be expected to find its way into the textbooks on social science research methodology and the major statistical packages.

REFERENCES

Andrich, D. (1988). Rasch models for measurement. *Sage University Paper Series on Quantitative Applications in the Social Sciences, 07-068.* Newbury Park, CA: Sage.

Andrich, D., & Luo, G. (1993). A hyperbolic cosine latent trait model for unfolding dichotomous single-stimulus responses. *Applied Psychological Measurement, 17,* 253–276.

Bond, T. G., & Fox, C. M. (2007). Applying the Rasch model. *Fundamental measurement in the social sciences.* Mahwah, NJ: Erlbaum.

Browne, M. (1992). Circumplex models for correlation matrices. *Psychometrika, 57,* 469–497.

Carroll, J. B. (1945). The effect of difficulty and chance success on correlations between items or between tests. *Psychometrika, 10,* 1–19.

Coombs, C. H. (1950). Psychological scaling without a unit of measurement. *Psychological Review, 57,* 145–158.

Coombs, C. H. (1964). *A theory of data.* New York, NY: Wiley.

Coombs, C. H., Dawes, R. M., & Tversky, A. (1970). *Mathematical psychology: An elementary introduction.* Englewood Cliffs, NJ: Prentice Hall.

Embretson, S., & Reise, S. P. (2000). *Item response theory for psychologists.* Mahwah, NJ: Erlbaum.

Ferguson, G. A. (1941). The factorial interpretation of test difficulty. *Psychometrika, 6,* 323–330.

Goodman, L. A., & Kruskal, W. H. (1979). *Measures of association for cross classifications.* New York, NY: Springer Verlag.

Guttman, L. (1950). The utility of scalogram analysis. In S. A. Stouffer, L. Guttman, E. A. Suchman, P. F. Lazarsfeld, S. A. Star, & J. A. Clausen (Eds.), *Measurement and prediction. Studies in Social Psychology in World War II* (Vol. 4, pp. 122–171). New York, NY: Wiley.

Huisman, M. (1998). *Item nonresponse: Occurrence, causes, and imputation of missing answers to test items.* Leiden, The Netherlands: DSWO Press.

Huisman, M. (2000). Imputation of missing item responses: Some simple techniques. *Quality and Quantity, 34,* 331–351.

Jacoby, W. G. (1991). Data theory and dimensional analysis. *Sage University Paper Series on Quantitative Applications in the Social Sciences, 07-078.* Newbury Park, CA: Sage.

Kingma, J., & Taerum, T. (1989). SPSS-X procedure and standalone programs for the Mokken scale analysis: A nonparametric item response theory model. *Educational & Psychological Measurement, 49,* 101–136.

Likert, R. (1932). A technique for the measurement of attitudes. *Archives of Psychology, 140,* 1–55.

Loevinger, J. (1948). The technique of homogeneous tests compared with some aspects of "scale analysis" and factor analysis. *Psychological Bulletin, 45,* 507–530.

McIver, J., & Carmines, E. G. (1981). Unidimensional scaling. *Sage University Paper Series on Quantitative Applications in the Social Sciences, 07-078.* Newbury Park, CA: Sage.

Meijer, R. R. (1994). The number of Guttman errors as a simple and powerful person-fit statistic. *Applied Psychological Measurement, 18,* 311–314.

Mokken, R. J. (1971). *A theory and procedure of scale analysis. With applications in political research.* Berlin, Germany: De Gruyter (Mouton).

Mokken, R. J. (1997). Nonparametric models for dichotomous responses. In W. J. van der Linden & R. K. Hambleton (Eds.), *Handbook of modern item response theory*. New York, NY: Springer Verlag.

Mokken, R. J., & Lewis, C. (1982). A nonparametrical approach to the analysis of dichotomous item responses. *Applied Psychological Measurement, 6*, 417–430.

Mokken, R. J., Lewis, C., & Sijtsma, K. (1986). Rejoinder to "The Mokken scale: A critical discussion". *Applied Psychological Measurement, 10*, 279–285.

Mokken, R. J., van Schuur, W. H., & Leeferink, A. J. (2001). The circles of our minds. A nonparametric IRT model for the circumplex. In A. Boomsma, M. A. J. van Duijn, & T. A. B. Snijders (Eds.), *Essays on item response theory* (pp. 339–356). New York, NY: Springer Verlag.

Molenaar, I. W. (1991). A weighted Loevinger **H**-coefficient extending Mokken scaling to multicategory items. *Kwantitatieve Methoden, 37*, 97–118.

Molenaar, I. W., & Sijtsma, K. (2000). User's manual MSP5 for Windows, A program for Mokken scale analysis for polytomous items, Version 5.0. Groningen, the Netherlands: Science Plus/iec ProGamma.

Molenaar, W. (1970). Approximations to the Poisson, binomial and hypergeometric distribution functions. MC Tract 31. Amsterdam, the Netherlands: Centrum voor Wiskunde en Informatica.

Niemöller, B., & van Schuur, W. H. (1983). Stochastic models for unidimensional scaling: Mokken and Rasch. In D. McKay, N. Schofield, & P. Whiteley (Eds.), *Data analysis and the social sciences* (pp. 120–170). London, England: Francis Pinter.

Ostini, R., & Nering, R. (2006). Polytomous item response theory models. *Sage University Paper Series on Quantitative Applications in the Social Sciences, 07-144*. Thousand Oaks, CA: Sage.

Plutchik, R., & Conte, H. R. (Eds.). (1997). *Circumplex models of personality and emotions*. Washington, DC: American Psychological Association.

Popper, K. R. (1959). *The logic of scientific discovery*. London, England: Hutchinson.

Popper, K. R. (2003). Conjectures and refutations. *The growth of scientific knowledge*. London, England: Routledge. (Original work published 1963)

Rasch, G. (1980). *Probabilistic models for some intelligence and attainment tests* (Copenhagen: Danish Institute for Educational Research), expanded edition. Chicago, IL: The University of Chicago Press. (Original work published 1960)

Roberts, J. S., Donoghue, J. R., & Laughlin, J. E. (2000). A general item response theory model for unfolding unidimensional polytomous responses. *Applied Psychological Measurement, 24*, 3–32.

Roskam, E. E., van den Wollenberg, A. L., & Jansen, P. G. W. (1986). The Mokken scale: A critical discussion. *Applied Psychological Measurement, 10*, 165–177.

Sanders, K., & Schuur, W. van. (1998). De Noorderlingen: Identiteit en Vertrouwen. *Sociale Wetenschappen, 41*, 24–48.

Sijtsma, K., & Molenaar, I. W. (2002). *Introduction to nonparametric item response theory*. Thousand Oaks, CA: Sage.

Smith, E. V., & Stone, G. E. (2009). *Criterion referenced testing: Practice analysis to score reporting using Rasch measurement*. Maple Grove, MN: Jam Press.

Van der Ark, L. A. (2007). *Mokken scale analysis in R. Journal of Statistical Software, 20*, 1–19.

van Schuur, W. H. (1993). Nonparametric unidimensional unfolding for multicategory data. *Political Analysis, 4*, 41–74.

van Schuur, W. H. (2003). Mokken scale analysis: Between the Guttman scale and parametric item response theory. *Political Analysis, 11*, 139–163.

van Schuur, W. H. & Kiers, H. A. L. (1994). Why factor analysis often is the wrong model for analyzing bipolar concepts and what model to use instead. *Applied Psychological Measurement, 18*, 97–110.

Weesie, J. (1999). MOKKEN: Stata module: Mokken scale analysis. Software Components RePEc:boc:bocode:sjw31, RePEc EconPapers. http://econpapers.repec.org/software/bocbocode/sjw31.htm

Wood, R. (1978). Fitting the Rasch model: A heady tale. *British Journal of Mathematical and Statistical Psychology, 31,* 27–32.

SELECTED BIBLIOGRAPHY

Ordinal IRT (Ordered by Year of Publication)

Molenaar, I. W. (1982). Mokken scaling revisited. *Kwantitatieve Methoden, 3*, 145–164.

Mokken, R. J., Lewis, C., & Sijtsma, K. (1986). Rejoinder to "The Mokken scale: A critical discussion." *Applied Psychological Measurement, 10*, 279–285.

Sijtsma, K., & Molenaar, I. W. (1987). Reliability of test scores in nonparametric item response theory. *Psychometrica, 52*, 79–97.

Sijtsma, K. (1988a). Reliability estimation in Mokken's nonparametric item response model. In W. E. Saris & I. N. Gallhofer (Eds.), *Sociometric research, Vol. I: Data collection and scaling* (pp. 159–174). London, England: MacMillan Press.

Sijtsma, K. (1988b). *Contributions to Mokken's nonparametric item response theory.* Amsterdam, The Netherlands: Free University Press.

Meijer, R. R., Sijtsma, K., & Smid, N. J. (1990). Theoretical and empirical comparison of the Mokken and the Rasch approach to IRT. *Applied Psychological Measurement, 14*, 283–298.

Sijtsma, K., Debets, P., & Molenaar, I. W. (1990). Using Mokken scale analysis to develop unidimensional scales. *Quality and Quantity, 24*, 173–188.

Hemker, B. T., Sijtsma, K., & Molenaar, I. W. (1995). Selection of unidimensional scales from a multidimensional item bank in the polytomous Mokken IRT model. *Applied Psychological Measurement, 19*, 337–352.

Sijtsma, K., & Junker, B. W. (1996). A survey of theory and methods of invariant item ordering. *British Journal of Mathematical and Statistical Psychology, 49*, 79–105.

Molenaar, I. W. (1997). Nonparametric models for polytomous responses. In W. J. Van der Linden & R. K. Hambleton (Eds.), *Handbook of modern item response theory* (pp. 369–380). New York, NY: Springer Verlag.

Sijtsma, K., & Hemker, B. T. (1998). Nonparametric polytomous IRT models for invariant item ordering, with results for parametric models. *Psychometrika, 63*, 183–200.

Van Abswoude, A. A. H., Vermunt, J. K., Hemker, B. T., & Van der Ark, L. A. (2004). Mokken scale analysis using hierarchical clustering procedures. *Applied Psychological Measurement, 28*, 332–354.

Software

Debets, P., Sijtsma, K., Brouwer, E., & Molenaar, I. W. (1988). MSP: A computer program for item analysis according to a nonparametric IRT approach. *Psychometrica, 54*, 534–536.

102

Kingma, J., & Reuvekamp, J. (1986). Mokken scale: A PASCAL program for non-parametric stochastic Mokken scales. *Educational and Psychological Measurement, 46,* 679–685.

Rivas, T., & Martinez, M. R. (1992). MOKPAS: Un programa para el escalamiento de items según el modelo TRI no paramétrico de Mokken. *Investigaciones Psicológicas,* 187–205.

Rivas, T., Martinez, M. R., & Hidalgo, R. (1996). MOKFOR1: A program to fit an accumulative scale to Mokken non parametric IRT model. 20th Biennial Conference of the Society for Multivariate Analysis in the Behavioral Sciences, ESADE, Barcelona.

Sijtsma, K., Debets, P., & Molenaar, I. W. (1990). Mokken scale analysis for polychotomous items: Theory, a computer program, and an empirical application. *Quality and Quantity, 24,* 173–188.

Applications

Barker, M., O'Hanlon, A., McGee, H. M., Hickey, A., & Conroy, R. M. (2007). Cross-sectional validation of the Aging Perceptions Questionnaire: A multidimensional instrument for assessing self-perceptions of aging. BMC Geriatrics, 7, 9.

Bech, P., Hansen, H. V., & Kessing, L. V. (2006). The internalising and externalising dimensions of affective symptoms in depressed (unipolar) and bipolar patients. *Psychotherapy and Psychosomatics, 75,* 362–369.

Boor, K., Scheele, F., van der Vleuten, C. P., Scherpbier, A. J., Teunissen, P. W., & Sijtsma, K. (2007). *Psychometric properties of an instrument to measure the clinical learning environment. Medical Education, 41,* 92–99.

Cingranelli, D. L., & Richards, D. L. (1999). Measuring the level, pattern and sequence of government respect for physical integrity rights. *International Studies Quarterly, 43,* 407–417.

Davenport, C. (1995). Multidimensional threat perception and state repression: An inquiry into why states apply negative sanctions. *American Journal of Political Science, 39,* 683–713.

de Jong, A., & Molenaar, I. W. (1987). An application of Mokken's model for stochastic, cumulative scaling in psychiatric research. *Journal of Psychiatric Research, 21,* 137–149.

Duivenvoorden, H. J., Tibboel, D., Koot, H. M., van Dijk, M., & Peters, J. W. (2006). Pain assessment in profound cognitive impaired children using the Checklist Pain Behavior: Is item reduction valid? *Pain, 126,* 147–154.

Ettema, T. P., Dröes, R. M., de Lange, J., Mellenbergh, G. J., & Ribbe, M. W. (2007). QUALIDEM: Development and evaluation of a dementia specific quality of life instrument. Scalability, reliability and internal structure. *International Journal of Geriatric Psychiatry, 22,* 549–556.

Gillespie, M., Tenvergert, E. M., & Kingma, J. (1987). Using Mokken scale analysis to develop unidimensional scales. Do the six abortion items in the NORC GSS form one or two scales? *Quality and Quantity, 21,* 393–408.

Gillespie, M., Tenvergert, E. M., & Kingma, J. (1988). Using Mokken methods to develop robust cross-national scales: American and West German attitudes toward abortion. *Social Indicators Research, 20,* 181–203.

Hosenfeld, B., Van den Boom, D. C., & Resing, W. C. M. (1997). Constructing geometric analogies for the longitudinal testing of elementary school children. *Journal of Educational Measurement, 34,* 367–372.

Ivarsson, B., & Malm, U. (2007). Self-reported consumer satisfaction in mental health services: Validation of a self-rating version of the UKU-Consumer Satisfaction Rating Scale. *Nordic Journal of Psychiatry, 61,* 194–200.

Jacoby, W. G. (1994). Public attitudes towards government spending. American *Journal of Political Science, 38,* 336–361.

Jacoby, W. G. (1995). The structure of ideological thinking in the American electorate. *American Journal of Political Science, 39,* 314–335.

Kingma, J., & Reuvekamp, J. (1984). The construction of a developmental scale for seriation. *Educational and Psychological Measurement, 44,* 1–23.

Kingma, J., & Te Vergert, E. M. (1985). A nonparametric scale analysis for the development of conservation. *Applied Psychological Measurement, 9,* 375–387.

Koh, C. L., Hsueh, I. P., Wang, W. C., Sheu, C. F., Yu, T. Y., Wang, C. H., & Hsieh, C. L. (2006). Validation of the action research arm test using item response theory in patients after stroke. *Journal of Rehabilitation Medicine, 38,* 375–380.

Kørner, A., Lauritzen, L., Abelskov, K., Gulmann, N. C., Brodersen, A. M., Wedervang-Jensen, T., & Marie Kjeldgaard, K. (2007). Rating scales for depression in the elderly: External and internal validity. *Journal of Clinical Psychiatry, 68,* 384–389.

Lecrubier, Y., & Bech, P. (2007). The Ham D(6) is more homogenous and as sensitive as the Ham D(17). *European Psychiatry, 22,* 252–255.

Licht, R. W., Qvitzau, S., Allerup, P., & Bech, P. (2005). Validation of the Bech–Rafaelsen Melancholia Scale and the Hamilton Depression Scale in patients with major depression: Is the total score a valid measure of illness severity? *Acta Psychiatrica Scandinavica, 111,* 144–149.

Luinge, M. R., Post, W. J., Wit, H. P., & Goorhuis-Brouwer, S. M. (2006). The ordering of milestones in language development for children from 1 to 6 years of age. *Journal of Speech, Language and Hearing Research, 49,* 923–940.

Olsen, L. R., Mortensen, E. L., & Bech, P. (2004). The SCL-90 and SCL-90R versions validated by item response models in a Danish community sample. *Acta Psychiatrica Scandinavica, 110,* 225–229.

Paas, L. J. (1998). Mokken scaling characteristic sets and acquisition patterns of durable and financial products. *Journal of Economic Psychology, 19,* 353–376.

Paas, L. J., & Molenaar, I. W. (2005). Analysis of acquisition patterns: A theoretical and empirical evaluation of alternative methods. *International Journal of Research in Marketing, 22,* 87–100.

Roorda, L. D., Roebroeck, M. E., van Tilburg, T., Lankhorst, G. J., & Bouter, L. M., Measuring Mobility Study Group. (2004). Measuring activity limitations in climbing stairs: Development of a hierarchical scale for patients with lower-extremity disorders living at home. *Archives of Physical Medicine and Rehabilitation, 85,* 967–971.

104

Scarritt, J. R. (1996). Measuring political change: The quantity and effectiveness of electoral and party participation in the Zambian one-party state, 1973–1991. *British Journal of Political Science, 26,* 283–297.

Schneider, S. K., Jacoby, W. G., & Coggburn, J. D. (1997). The structure of bureaucratic decisions in the American states. *Public Administration Review, 57,* 240–249.

Segura, S. L., & Gonzalez-Roma, V. (2003). How do subjects construe ambiguous response formats of affect items? *Journal of Personality and Social Psychology, 85,* 956–968.

Sijtsma, K., Emons, W. H., Bouwmeester, S., Nyklícek, I., & Roorda, L. D. (2008). Nonparametric IRT analysis of quality-of-life scales and its application to the World Health Organization Quality-of-Life Scale (WHOQOL-Bref). *Quality of Life Research, 17,* 275–290.

Sijtsma, K., & Verwey, A. (1992). Mokken scale analysis: Theoretical considerations and an application to transitivity tasks. *Applied Measurement in Education, 5,* 355–373.

Stochl, J., Boomsma, A., van Duijn, M., Brozová, H., & Růzická, E. (2008). Mokken scale analysis of the UPDRS: Dimensionality of the Motor Section revisited. 1. *Neuro Endocrinology Letters, 29,* 151–158.

Van der Putten, A., Vlaskamp, C., Reynders, K., & Nakken, H. (2005). Movement skill assessment in children with profound multiple disabilities: A psychometric analysis of the top down motor milestone test. *Clinical Rehabilitation, 19,* 635–643.

Van der Veer, K., Ommundsen, R., Larsen, K. S., Le, H. V., Krumov, K., Pernice, R. E., & Romans, G. P. (2004). Structure of attitudes toward illegal immigration: Development of cross-national cumulative scales. *Psychological Reports, 94,* 897–906.

van Schuur, W. H., & Vis, J. C. P. M. (2000). What Dutch parliamentary journalists know about politics. *Acta Politica, 35,* 196–227.

Verweij, A. C., Sijtsma, K., & Koops, W. (1996). A Mokken scale for transitive reasoning suited for longitudinal research. *International Journal of Behavioral Development, 19,* 219–238.

Watson, R., Deary, I. J., & Shipley, B. (2008). A hierarchy of distress: Mokken scaling of the GHQ-30. *Psychological Medicine, 38,* 575–579.

Zinn, F. D., Henderson, D. A., Nystuen, J. D., & Drake, W. D. (1992). A stochastic cumulative scaling method applied to measuring wealth in Indonesian villages. *Environment and Planning A, 24,* 1155–1166.

APPENDIX 1

The Null Distribution of the **H** *Coefficient*

It is possible to estimate the probability that a certain value of the coefficient of homogeneity (say, 0.50) in a sample of size N is found in a population that has an **H** coefficient of 0.00. To estimate that probability, we need the distribution of the **H** coefficient in the case that all responses are statistically independent. In a 2×2 table with fixed marginals we can calculate $\mathbf{H}(ij)$ not only on the basis of the error cell but also on the basis of the $(1,1)$ cell:

$$\mathbf{H}(ij) = \frac{p(ij) - p(i) * p(j)}{p(i) * [1 - p(j)]}, \text{ or } \frac{\Delta(ij)}{p(i) * [1 - p(j)]}$$

Mokken derived the distribution of **H**: The mean is 0.00, and the variance depends on the difficulties of the items and can be written as follows (Mokken 1971, p. 162):

$$\sigma^2 = p(i)[1 - p(i)]p(j)[1 - p(j)]$$

So the standard deviation σ of this distribution is its square root.

Mokken defined $\Delta(ij)^* = \sqrt{(N-1)} * \Delta(ij)/\sigma$, which has a standard normal distribution for large enough N. In later publications, $\Delta(ij)^*$ was redefined as $Z(ij)$. So if the $Z(ij)$ score is larger than 1.64, then the probability that the coefficient of homogeneity observed is larger than 0.00 in the entire population is more than 5%, as is a common (one sided) interpretation with standard normal distributions. We will use Table 5.2 (chapter 5) to illustrate the calculation of $Z(ij)$:

	0	1	Total	
0	157	*134*	291	24.25%
1	185	724	909	75.75%
Total	342	858	1,200	
	28.5%	71.5%		

Table A.1 Life (horizontal) by Hell (vertical).

$$p(ij) = 724/1,200 = 60.33\% \quad p(i) = 0.7575 \quad p(j) = 0.715$$
$$p(i) * p(j) = 0.5416$$

$$\Delta(ij) = p(ij) - [p(i) * p(j)] = 0.6033 - 0.5416 = 0.0617$$

$$\sigma^2 = (0.2425 * 0.7575 * 0.285 * 0.715) = 0.0374, \text{ so } \sigma = 0.1934$$

$$\sqrt{(1,200 - 1)} = \sqrt{1,199} = 34.627; \; 34.627 * 0.0617 = 2.136;$$
$$2.136/0.1934 = 11.05$$

So $\Delta(ij)^*$ or $Z(ij) = 11.05$. This is much larger than 3, so the $H(ij)$ value is highly significant.

Note that Mokken compared the observed and expected value of the (1,1) or (+,+) cell and not the observed and expected value of the error cell. But a 2×2 table with given marginals has only one degree of freedom, so it does not make a difference whether the error cell is evaluated or the (1,1) cell.

A **Z** value for the whole scale can be calculated as $\mathbf{Z} =$

$$\mathbf{Z} = \frac{\sqrt{(N-1)} \sum_{i=1}^{k-1} \sum_{j=i+1}^{k} \Delta(ij)}{\sqrt{\sum_{i=1}^{k-1} \sum_{j=i+1}^{k} \sigma ij^2}}$$

$Z(i)$ values for individual items can be found in the same way, by summing $\Delta(ij)$ and σij^2) only over the Δs and σs that contain item i.

APPENDIX 2

Preventing Capitalizing on Chance

When new items enter in the scale, we want to make the criteria for entering increasingly strict. We do this by making the criterion for statistical significance increasingly strict. Initially, each item has to have an $H(i)$ value that is significantly larger than 0. In order to do this we use the z score that is based on the standard deviation of the **H** coefficient in a population with $\mathbf{H} = 0$. We then use a user-defined level of confidence, or rather an α level, as its complement, generally 5%. When the scale becomes larger, we want to reduce that probability from, say, 5% to increasingly lower numbers (α^*) so as to increase the level of confidence. Mokken suggested the following procedure.

1. Select a general level of confidence $1 - \alpha$ (where, e.g., $\alpha = 0.05$).

2. Rather than using this alpha level, use an adapted α level (α^*) that divides the user-specified level by the number of item pairs $[\alpha^* = \alpha/\frac{1}{2}(n - 1)n]$.

3. With the inclusion of each additional item to the scale, increase the denominator by some value $k(r_j)$, where r_j is the number of remaining items at step j from among which the next selection is to be made. The start set is used at step 1, and the first additional item is added at step 2. The test for the selection of the $(j - 1)$-th additional item, when h steps have already been made, is then computed at confidence level:

$$\alpha^* = \frac{\alpha}{\frac{1}{2}(n-1)n + \displaystyle\sum_{j=2}^{h} r_j}$$

Let us make this procedure clear with an example. Suppose that 10 items are all positively correlated and may form part of a cumulative scale and that the user-selected alpha level is 0.05. With 10 items there are 45 item pairs, so the α^* level used for the evaluation of the first pair is $0.05/45 = 0.00111$. After the first item pair is selected, a third item will be chosen from among the 8 remaining items. This means that the α^* level used for the evaluation of the third item in the existing two-item scale is $0.05/(45 + 8) = 0.00094$. For the selection of a fourth item the α^* level used will be $0.05/(45 + 8 + 7)$ $= 0.00083$, and so on. In many practical applications, when the number of subjects in the sample is not too small (e.g., greater than 100) and when the item difficulties are not too extreme (e.g., between 0.1 and 0.9), this preventive measure does not affect the outcome.

APPENDIX 3

Calculation of Reliability

The probability of giving the same response twice, as is required in a test–retest reliability, is generally not obtained by asking the same question twice. Mokken suggested obtaining this probability by using the P(+,+) matrix, which gives the proportion of subjects who give the positive response to pairs of items. If the items conform to the requirement of double monotonicity, then the proportions of positive responses in the P(+,+) matrix will increase from left to right and from top to bottom, when the items are ordered according to their difficulty. The diagonal cells can then be interpreted as the proportion of subjects who would have given the positive response to the same item twice ($p(ii)$). These proportions can be obtained by extrapolation (for the first and last item) or interpolation (for the intermediate items). Let us use our example of American religious beliefs. The diagonal values of the P(+,+) matrix give these extrapolated or interpolated values (marked with an asterisk).

Item	P	A = Hell	B = Life	C = Heaven	D = Soul	E = God
		0.71	0.76	0.85	0.94	0.94
A = Hell	0.71	0.58*	0.60	0.71	0.71	0.71
B = Life	0.76	0.60	0.64*	0.70	0.75	0.74
C = Heaven	0.85	0.71	0.70	0.78*	0.83	0.84
D = Soul	0.94	0.71	0.75	0.83	0.91*	0.91
E = God	0.94	0.71	0.74	0.84	0.91	0.91*

Table A.2 P(+,+) matrix, ++ probabilities, and estimation of reliability.

Extrapolating the value for item E is based on the assumption that the relation between the marginal difficulties of the items immediately preceding item E (their $p(i)$ values) is the same as the relation between the proportion of positive responses to the item pairs with these immediately preceding items. So

$$\text{Extrapolation for } p(\text{EE}): \frac{p(\text{E}) - p(\text{C})}{p(\text{D}) - p(\text{C})} = \frac{p(\text{EE}) - p(\text{CE})}{p(\text{DE}) - p(\text{CE})}$$

If we work this out we get $(0.94 - 0.85)/(0.94 - 0.85) = [p(\text{EE}) - 0.84]/(0.91 - 0.84)$.

Or $p(\text{EE}) = 0.91$.

$$\text{Interpolation for } p(\text{BB}): \frac{p(\text{C}) - p(\text{B})}{p(\text{C}) - p(\text{A})} = \frac{p(\text{BC}) - p(\text{BB})}{p(\text{BC}) - p(\text{AB})}$$

If we work this out we get $(0.85 - 0.76)/(0.85 - 0.71) = [0.70 - p(\text{BB})]/(0.70 - 0.60)$.

Or $p(\text{BB}) = 0.64$.

The estimates of these diagonal elements are now used in a formula for the reliability, which Mokken derived (formula 2.28, in section 4.4.2, p. 145 in Mokken, 1971). The numerator in this formula is an estimate of the variance of the true score, and the denominator is an estimate of the variance of the observed score. Sijtsma and Molenaar (1987) show that this method compares favorably with other methods of establishing reliability.

$$\text{Reliability} = \frac{\sum_{i=1}^{k} [p(ii) - p(i)^2] + 2 \sum_{i=1}^{k-1} \sum_{j=i+1}^{k} [p(ij) - p(i) * p(j)]}{\sum_{i=1}^{k} [p(i)(1 - p(i))] + 2 \sum_{i=1}^{k-1} \sum_{j=i+1}^{k} [p(ij) - p(i) * p(j)]}$$

As in most reliability analyses, reliability increases as the number of (homogeneous) items increases. A short scale (with few items) can have a high homogeneity and a low reliability. Reliabilities over 0.60 are advisable for accepting a set of items as a scale in a survey.

AUTHOR INDEX

111

SUBJECT INDEX

SAGE Research Methods Online

The essential tool for researchers

Sign up now at www.sagepub.com/srmo for more information.

An expert research tool

- An **expertly designed taxonomy** with more than 1,400 unique terms for social and behavioral science research methods

- **Visual and hierarchical search tools** to help you discover material and link to related methods

- Easy-to-use navigation tools
- Content organized by complexity
- Tools for citing, printing, and downloading content with ease
- Regularly updated content and features

A wealth of essential content

- The most comprehensive picture of quantitative, qualitative, and mixed methods available today

- More than **100,000 pages of SAGE book and reference material** on research methods as well as editorially selected material from SAGE journals

- More than **600 books** available in their entirety online

Launching 2011!

$SAGE research methods online